Sand, Wind, and War

Sand, Wind, and War

MEMOIRS OF A DESERT EXPLORER

RALPH A. BAGNOLD

The University of Arizona Press
Tucson

The University of Arizona Press
www.uapress.arizona.edu

© 1990 by The Arizona Board of Regents
All rights reserved. Published 1990
Century Collection edition 2019

ISBN-13: 978-0-8165-1211-9 (cloth)
ISBN-13: 978-0-8165-3949-9 (Century Collection paper)

Library of Congress Cataloging-in-Publication Data
Bagnold, Ralph A. (Ralph Alger), 1896–1990
    Sand, wind, and war : memoirs of a desert explorer / Ralph A. Bagnold
        p. cm.
    Includes index.
    ISBN 0-8165-1211-6 (cl. : alkaline paper)
    1. Bagnold, Ralph A. (Ralph Alger), 1896–1990. 2. Explorers—Great
Britain—Biography. I. Title.
G246.B33A3 1990
509.2—dc20
    [B]   90 – 46430
                                                              CIP

Printed in the United States of America
♾ This paper meets the requirements of ANSI/NISO Z39.48-1992
(Permanence of Paper).

To the memory of my late wife, "Plankie,"
and to our son Stephen and
daughter Jane McKenzie.

Contents

Foreword   ix

Preface   xiii

ONE Early Days
1

TWO France and Flanders: 1915–1918
23

THREE Cambridge: 1919–1921
35

FOUR Ireland: 1921–1923
43

FIVE Egypt: 1926–1929
49

SIX India: 1928–1931
73

SEVEN Family and an Expedition to the Sudan: 1931–1932
81

EIGHT   The Far East: 1933–1934
91

NINE   Physics of Blown Sand: 1935–1939
103

TEN   Second World War: 1939–1944
119

ELEVEN   Lyminge—Marriage—Shell: 1944–1949
145

TWELVE   Rickwoods—Egyptian Fantasia—Algeria— Kuwait: 1949–1952
153

THIRTEEN   Physicists and Engineers—A Basic Experiment: 1953–1958
161

FOURTEEN   Luna Leopold—Washington, D.C.: 1956–1964
165

FIFTEEN   With Leopold in Wyoming: 1967–1974
173

SIXTEEN   Meanwhile and Elsewhere: 1966–1974
181

SEVENTEEN   Later: 1974–1986
189

Index
201

Foreword

IT IS UNUSUAL to find a professional soldier who is known primarily for his contributions to intellectual and scientific thought. This is true, however, of Brigadier Ralph A. Bagnold, whose research spanned several of the physical sciences, including hydrology, geophysics, oceanography, and geography. His earliest scientific publications appeared in the 1930s and dealt with the movement of desert sand; his two last papers were in 1983 and 1986, respectively examining the random distributions of word lengths and sediment transport in water. This productivity and originality seems astonishing when one considers that Bagnold was not formally trained as a scientist and had never been a professional academician.

Sand, Wind, and War is Bagnold's account of his life, starting with experiences as a youth that instilled in him a curiosity about places and things. The account of his youth does much to explain how he made the transition from professional soldier to scientist. Commissioned as a regular officer in the Royal Engineers in 1915, Bagnold served in the trenches of France and Flanders during World War I. After the war, he took time out from the army to earn an honors degree in engineering at Cambridge and then rejoined the army, serving in Egypt, India, and China. While stationed in Egypt, he and other young officers began tinkering with Model-T and Model-A Fords, modifying them in ways similar to those that youngsters in California would use in the 1960s and later to design "dune buggies." Gradually this tinkering led to a more serious interest in exploring the dunes, and during periods of leave they organized trips into the surrounding desert country. Such trips developed into serious large-scale geographic exploration of the last remaining unmapped areas of the earth. They developed techniques for taking these simple cars deep into the dune country, inventing ingenious devices to keep themselves from becoming stranded in these remote seas of sand.

Bagnold learned from experience what part of a dune would support the car and where the wheels would sink in. This was the beginning of a growing knowledge about dunes and the movement of sand. As his young friends were gradually reassigned elsewhere, Bagnold turned his attention to examining the processes by which dunes are formed and maintained. His retirement from the Royal Army in 1935 allowed him to devote full time to laboratory experiments designed to interpret his observations in the desert. The results were published in 1941 in a book which remains the classic in the field today, *The Physics of Blown Sand and Desert Dunes.* Meanwhile, he published a delightful chronicle of his explorations entitled *Libyan Sands,* a book filled with his zest for adventure and his keen eye for detail.

As Britain was plunged into World War II, Bagnold was recalled to the Royal Army. In 1939 he was en route to an unexciting posting in East Equatorial Africa when his ship was involved in a collision and had to put in to Port Said for repairs. His presence in Egypt came to the attention of the commanding general for that region, who knew of Bagnold's experience in the desert and quickly had his orders changed. Bagnold was given a free hand to develop the Long Range Desert Group, an unconventional "private army" that traveled undetected through remote regions of the desert to harass the enemy with unexpected attacks. So important and useful was the work of the Long Range Desert Group that Bagnold rose to the rank of brigadier and directed the operations from headquarters. He retired again in 1944, and after a few years as Director of Research for Shell Oil, he once more took up his principal hobby of studying the transport of sand. Now he extended his work beyond the movement of sand by wind to include grains moved in any fluid.

In the latter chapters of *Sand, Wind, and War* Bagnold discusses his philosophy and approach to scientific research. The position of importance he has earned in science stems from his insistence on critical experimentation combined with the use of pure physics. His goal was to eliminate the empiricism that so long dominated the problem of transportation of debris in water. This led to a productive association with the U.S. Geological Survey, which published a series of his papers, the most important being a 1966 Professional Paper entitled "An Approach to the Sediment Transport Problem from General Physics." In the field of oceanography he studied the motion of sand on beaches and the hydraulics of submarine density currents.

Although Bagnold still tended to view himself as an amateur, he was accorded the highest honors of professional societies. In geography, his explorations in Libya won him the Founders' Gold Medal of the Royal Geographical Society; in hydraulics and related fields, he was given the G. K. Warren Prize of the National Academy of Sciences, the Penrose Medal of the Geological Society of America, and the Sorby Medal of the International Association of Sedimentologists. However, Bagnold must have taken greatest pleasure in being elected a Fellow of the Royal Society. He recounts that even early in his military career he expressed to his sister that he would rather be an FRS than a brigadier general. It is a measure of his accomplishments that he managed both.

Bagnold had many fascinating experiences, both as an explorer and in the military, and he had much to share concerning his views on scientific research. We are fortunate that he completed his autobiography shortly before his death in May 1990. Those who knew

him only through his research papers can now come to appreciate
the total wealth of his experience.

LUNA B. LEOPOLD

PAUL D. KOMAR

VANCE HAYNES

June 1990

Preface

SINCE I WAS born, now nearly a century ago, more changes in our life-styles have occurred than in any other period of written history—flying, nuclear power, space travel, motor transport, television, X-rays, and plastics, to name but a few. Sadly, the faster the rate of change, the faster memory fades into vague legend and soon into oblivion. With this in mind, I set out to write a private family record of my own life. So many latent memories began to emerge, however, of so diverse and so unusual a nature, that I decided the story might be of wider interest.

From an early age I have been aware of an urge to see and do things new and unique—to explore the unknown or to explain the inexplicable in natural science. Providence has granted me an opportunity to fulfill these urges to some degree. My life has been interspersed with a number of interesting and unusual episodes, some of which I share with you on the following pages.

I am very grateful to Luna B. Leopold for suggesting many valuable amplifications in the earlier chapters and for compiling the necessary maps, and to Vance Haynes for having the maps drafted and for supplying some of the photographs. My sincere thanks are also due to Paul D. Komar for his kindly diligence in piecing my amended story together.

RALPH A. BAGNOLD

April 1990

2

Early Days

AMONG MY EARLIEST memories are an ornamental grotto with a little waterfall at the back on the grounds of my grandparents' home and seeing the tangle of service pipes high up at the back of the house. Possibly one's earliest retained memories may presage future interests. The pipes certainly did in my case. The grotto, too, which I was prevented from entering, may have signified a latent craving to explore.

I was born on Good Friday, the third of April 1896, at the Manor House, Stoke, Devonport, the home of my mother's parents. My grandfather, William Henry Alger, was a businessman, twice mayor of Plymouth, and a partner in the firm of Burnard and Alger, which manufactured chemical fertilizers at a factory and wharf on the Cattewater Inlet of Plymouth Sound. The partnership between the families of Burnard and Alger was to last for three generations. Together with the continuing ties it forged with South Devon and the Alger family, this partnership had an appreciable influence, ultimately financial, on my life.

The Algers had four children, my uncles Harold (the eldest) and Archy, my mother, Ethel, and Aunt Edie. The family was old-fashioned "South Devon"—comfortably off, with plenty of good food, cream, and hospitality.

My father, Major (later Colonel) Arthur Henry Bagnold of the Royal Engineers (1854–1944), had no county ties. His parents, many years dead, had both been associated with the Honorable East India Company (HEIC). His father, Major General Michael Edward Bagnold (1786–1857) had served in the company's army. After thirty-one years of continuous service in India and its dependencies, he returned to England in 1835 on a three-year furlough. Immediately before returning to India, he proposed (by the then-new "electric telegraph") and was accepted by Eliza Larkins Walker, whose mother's family, the Larkins, had for several generations been shipowners in the East India Company's armed merchant fleet. There being no time to get a passage for her in the same ship, the bride-to-be followed on a venturesome journey to India by the new "overland route" that involved ship passage to Alexandria, Nile craft to Cairo, three days' caravan journey across the desert to Suez, and finally a ship to Bombay (the Suez Canal was not opened until 1858, after which this overland route was abandoned). My grandparents were married in Bombay in 1838.

Grandfather Bagnold finally retired in 1846, eleven years before the mutiny of the Bengal army. The Great Indian Mutiny, as it was called, came as a profound shock to the British government and people. Many English were murdered, including a great-aunt of mine. The mutiny was confined largely to the Bengal army and was put down by loyal troops from other provinces, led by British officers whose deeds became famous. Grandfather died that same year at his home, Hamilton Terrace, in London. With the Great Indian Mutiny there ended that strange anachronism whereby a self-perpetuating group of London businessmen, the Court of Directors of the HEIC, governed India from the city of London. Protected from foreign interference by their own large army and armed merchant navy, they controlled an empire of several hundred million people in the name of the Mogul emperors who continued to hold a feeble court in Delhi. After the mutiny, the whole of the peninsula came under the British Crown, acting through its viceroy. Earlier, Sir Arthur Wellesley, afterwards created first duke of Wellington, had been hired or borrowed from the East India Company by the British government to command the army that finally defeated Napoleon at the Battle of Waterloo. He had previously been a successful general in the company's "Indian Army."

I sometimes find it hard to realize that my own grandfather, my father's father, was born before the French Revolution and the Napoleonic Wars, and before the United States, as such, came into being. Three generations have now spanned two centuries, from 1786 to the present. General Michael Bagnold's brother, my great-uncle Tom, was born seven years earlier, in 1780. He joined the British navy and may well have served for a short time as an officer in Nelson's fleet. After leaving home, the two brothers did not see one another for forty years.

My grandmother Eliza Bagnold (1817–1873), who was considerably younger than my grandfather, lived on with the family in Hamilton Terrace until my father was nineteen. My aunt Alice, the eldest, later married the Reverend John Clay, rector of Ambleside near Windermere in the Lake District. She had eleven children—two boys, Owen and Arundel, and nine girls, none of whom either married or escaped from the heavy clerical atmosphere. Owen migrated to Canada. Arundel became a civil engineer, and I kept in touch with him, on and off, until he died in 1981 at the age of eighty-nine. There was also my uncle Lexy (Alexander Burns Bagnold), named after Sir Alexander Burns, a diplomat murdered in Afghanistan who had been a close friend of my grandfather. Lexy, who remained a bachelor, became a barrister and was for many years secretary to the Joint Fire Offices Committee of the insurance industry. As children we were very fond of Uncle Lexy. He used to talk solemn nonsense to us with a straight face. Aunt Clara, who also never married, kept house for her brother until her death shortly before the First World War. During that war a zeppelin bomb fell on Lexy's ground-floor flat in Maida Vale, London, blowing him, then aged between sixty-five and seventy, into the street, peppered with splintered glass but otherwise undamaged.

My father, the youngest (1854–1944), was born when my grandfather was in his sixty-eighth year and within three years of his death. Destined, in Eliza's mind, for the army, he was sent to Cheltenham College. Thence, having passed the army entrance exam with sufficiently high marks, he became a "gentleman cadet" at the Royal Military Academy, Woolwich (reserved for the engineers and artillery). After two years at the academy and a further two years as a "young officer" at the School of Military Engineering at Chatham, he was gazetted lieutenant, Royal Engineers, in 1872. Horatio Herbert Kitchener, also an engineers officer, was a contemporary. According to my father, Kitchener was then a dreamy, aloof young man, referred to as "Old Kitch" and thought rather dull. Years later Kitchener emerged as the organizer and commander of the Anglo-Egyptian army which reconquered the Sudan in 1898. A popular hero, he became Lord Kitchener of Khartoum. Later still, he became war secretary in 1914 and raised "Kitchener's Army" of volunteers.

My father's first independent job (1878–1880) seems to have been in Cyprus constructing a pipeline water supply to the town of Limasol. On a brief visit to the mainland he found Kitchener firmly established as director of the Palestine Survey, summoning subordinates by a clap of the hands. A local contractor named Z. Z. Williamson, referred to as Zealous Zachariah, was employed on the pipeline job. It seems that the same man emerged thirty-five years later as Sir Basil Zaharoff, an important figure in the shady background of Lloyd George's war financing.

In 1881–82 my father saw active service with the Telegraph Battalion in South Africa during the first Boer War. He got a letter of congratulation from the chief of staff which I will refer to again later. He saw active service once more in 1884–85, also with a telegraph unit, when he took part in the abortive Nile expedition to rescue General Gordon at Khartoum. Thomas Cook's Nile steamers were used as transports together with towed lighters which had to be hauled up over the cataracts by columns of soldiers on the riverbank. A naval gunboat was included, commanded by Lieutenant

Beatty, later Admiral Beatty of Battle of Jutland fame. The expedition forced its way upriver through some six hundred miles of then unknown desert, open to attack by dervishes at any time.

By custom, Thomas Cook's steamers carried a reserve of mummies as a specially fast-burning fuel for emergencies such as difficult cataracts. My father once heard the captain shout to his engine room staff, "All right, throw on another pharaoh."

They reached Khartoum two days too late. The city had fallen. Gordon had been killed.

My father stayed on in Egypt till 1887 with the Frontier Field Force, which was deployed for the defense of Upper Egypt against dervish raids from the south. During that time he and his men were borrowed by Dr. Wallis Budge, the leading Egyptologist of that era. Among other jobs, my father succeeded in raising intact the colossal statue of Ramses II that had been lying for eons in a pool of mud. With the aid of hydraulic jacks, they lifted it to its presently prone but decently housed position in the village of Bedrashain on the site of ancient Memphis. It was said that Budge smuggled the bulkier antiquities out of Egypt to the British Museum by organizing funeral flotillas, complete with mourners, down to Alexandria. This no doubt took place to the reward and amusement of the villagers concerned. He taught my father many useful things, including how to enter an already opened tomb: "Always send a native in first to absorb the fleas."

A good portion of a Royal Engineer officer's service in peacetime is spent in maintaining or modifying War Department buildings and other permanent structures, including coastal defense forts at home and abroad. Early in 1888 my father, then Major Bagnold, was posted for such employment to Plymouth. There he met, courted, and later the same year married my mother, Ethel. Her diary records much intimate detail of their years together. In the following year he was re-posted to Chatham, where he shortly became instructor in electricity at the School of Military Engineering. My sister Enid (1889–1981) was born on 27 October. She was to become a famous writer, best known for the children's classic *National Velvet* and for the play *The Chalk Garden*. Her autobiography was published in 1969.

Father remained at Chatham for the unusually long period of seven years, until early in 1896. In that year he became involved in the development and installation of a new coast defense weapon, the Brennan torpedo. This project involved a good deal of travel, including visits to overseas fortresses such as Gibraltar and Malta. My mother went to stay with her parents at the Manor House, Devonport, for my birth in April. By luck, or more likely by a wangle, my father was posted to Devonport that same year. He remained there for three years, until 1899.

It was during this torpedo interlude that my father became a close friend of the inventor Louis Brennan. According to my father, Brennan happened to be playing in his bath with one of his wife's reels of cotton. He noticed that as he pulled the cotton toward him, the reel went away from him. This was the basis of the Brennan torpedo, whose only working parts were a pair of drums of fine piano wire, each attached to a propeller. The wires led side by side to winding drums ashore. The Brennan torpedo had two great advantages: it could be steered by winding in one wire faster than the other, and it left no visible trail of bubbles. But alas, in practice it was found to have insufficient range and was soon replaced by the more conventional Whitehead torpedo driven by compressed air.

With his knowledge of Egypt and the upper Nile, my father must have been sad not to take part in Kitchener's 1897–98 campaign to reconquer the Sudan from the dervishes. But active service had to be fairly shared out. Moreover, it was evident that the major engineering job would be railway construction, of which he had no experience. At the same time he had a serious decision to make. Having recently taken part, as one of the British delegates, in an international conference of electrical engineers in San Francisco, he was asked to be vice president and ultimately president of the Institution of Electrical Engineers. But he had his army career to think of. He was about to be promoted, and there was then no senior job for a specialist in electrical applications. He reluctantly decided to refuse the vice presidency of the institution. Now that electricity enters into every aspect of civilization, it hardly seems credible that ninety years ago, a mere lifetime, there was so little knowledge of it that a serving army major could have been selected to preside over a national institution composed mainly of industrialists.

In May 1899 the family embarked in a steamship for Jamaica— Lieutenant Colonel Bagnold, my mother, my sister Enid (aged nine), myself (just three), and a French nursery governess. I remember only two things about that voyage: being knocked down on deck by a flying fish, and the roar of live steam from the boilers let in to heat the seawater in the bath.

My father's office in Jamaica, and the Royal Engineers' yard with its building materials and equipment, were down on the coastal plain near Kingston. For the family he rented Coldspring House up on a steep hillside in the cool Blue Mountains. The house, formerly a coffee mill, was divided inside by a chasm where a big waterwheel had once turned. Outside, in tiers, were the barbecues—low-walled concrete floors where the coffee berries were once dried in the sun. There was the Negro cook, Mrs. Pascow, fat and smiling, and Old Zink the groom. There must have been other Negro servants too, all descendants of African slaves. (The original Caribs of the West Indies had long since been exterminated by the Spanish and British.) We also had a two-horse carriage, used mainly for shopping in the little garrison town of Newcastle some miles farther up the winding mountain road. Father kept another horse at his office, which he used to ride to Coldspring House to be with us for weekends.

Looking out from the altitude of Coldspring House, I could see the whole of Kingston Harbor. There was a good view of the crater of a submerged volcano, with the water entering through a gap in the seaward rim. At one end of the gap lay the old settlement of Port Royal, once a base of the pirate Captain Morgan.

I remember quite a lot about my life at Coldspring House, some of it no doubt contemporary hearsay from my parents' talk. An early memory is of sitting on my pot in the nursery and being made to shout "J'ai fini, Mademoiselle." How I hated French then.

Once some people came to stay with us, bringing a baby raw with general eczema and a nurse fresh out from England. My mother carefully showed the nurse how to protect the child's cot from ants by standing the legs in paraffin [kerosene], as all our furniture was protected. She did three legs herself, leaving the fourth for the nurse. That night the household was roused by screams. Cot and child were black with ants. The nurse had disdained to treat the remaining cot leg. Curiously, in a day or so the eczema had gone. I developed a lasting revulsion to ants. I once watched my father, in his dressing gown, making a gimlet hole in the boarded ceiling. As soon as he pulled the gimlet out, before he could escape, a continuous black jet of ants poured down over his head.

Coldstream was a paradise for children. The mossy woods were carpeted with wild strawberries. We could pick an orange or a banana off a tree at will, or chew coffee berries, spitting out the beans. My mother used to make realistic little villages for us from moss and fallen twigs. But Enid, being six and a half years older, played with me rather reluctantly. The age gap prevented our being really close. I remember that she had a pony named Queeny. One or two of the young officers of the Newcastle garrison made a pet of her now and then, and once, as a treat, she was allowed to mount a real polo pony. She doted on ponies and riding. She used to gallop about holding a little cardboard bridle in front of her. In her eyes I was just "my little brother," so I was left much to my own devices.

Daddy once let me rummage about in the Royal Engineers' supply yard. I found some old water-pipe fittings which screwed together and which I was allowed to take home, and big drainpipes— tees, bends, and traps—which he explained the use of. He also gave

me some cement and a trowel and showed me how to make concrete.

I was obsessed by pipes, probably because of the same underlying pleasure in their continuity that one gets from model railways,
and possibly stimulates archaeologists to trace the long backward
extension of time. I learned to make complete models of household
drainage systems in plasticine [modeling clay]. I was given plenty
of plasticine. In that warm climate it remained soft and easily
worked. I would roll it into thin sheets, cut them into strips, and roll
these lengthwise around a pencil. With a little moulded collar on
one end, the pipes fitted together nicely. I moulded little W.C.s [toi-
lets] and joined them to the main drain, delighted with my achievement when water ran through the system without a leak. A small
streamlet ran above the house, a relic of the supply to the old waterwheel. With Daddy's encouragement I dammed it and diverted
the water into a new cemented channel. No doubt he was pleased to
see his son learning something of hydraulics. For my fifth birthday
I asked for and was given a cold chisel and a hammer to cut a water
channel through the surface of a small rock outcrop. I once mis-
judged, and water poured into the house, but I proudly rectified
matters with cement.

To my mother I must have been a messy child. As a Royal Engineers officer my father was trained to earn his men's respect by
acquiring a working knowledge of all their trades. He was determined that I should be brought up in the same persuasion. He had
inherited from his father a fine set of carpenter's tools in a great
chest made in India long ago and, like all of General Michael's belongings, designed to be carried by an elephant. My father also had
a large set of metal-working tools. He could make, mend, or improvise almost anything.

We left Jamaica for England in March 1902. I had my sixth birthday
during the voyage, and the captain had a birthday cake made for
me. After trying to cut it, I was stood up in the captain's chair in

front of all the first-class passengers and recited "The agèd, agèd man, asitting on a gate." Before I had finished, there was a shout from deck and everyone trooped up to watch a whale blowing, sending great jets of water high into the air. The ship's course ran through part of the Sargasso Sea where the weeds floated in dense masses on oily, waveless water. The faint memory reminds me of the Ancient Mariner: "The very sea did rot, dear God, that this should ever be. Yea, slimy things did crawl with legs upon the slimy sea."

England seemed a new world. The old queen had died; her reign had spanned most people's lives. The Sudan was being quietly re-settled after the fourteen-year horror of the dervish anarchy; half the population had died of war, famine, or pestilence. The South African war was over. In the streets I saw for the first time strange vehicles that moved by themselves, without any horse. Some were clearly driven by steam like railway engines, but others made a funny popping noise. I was told vaguely that these had oil engines. I failed to understand how even the most slippery oil could produce power to drive the things. Many houses were lit by the newfangled "piped gas." It burned with a naked yellow fish-tail flame that hissed.

My father was posted temporarily to the Isle of Wight, and we lived in a rented house in Ryde. I remember little of that year. There was a public canoe pond; I was taken to Shanklyn Chine with its coloured sands and to Carisbrook Castle where a goat was busy eating a newspaper. The following year, 1903, my father became a full colonel, in charge of all the buildings, roads, and railways in Woolwich Arsenal and at the explosives factory at Waltham Abbey.

Father bought Warren Wood, a house with about two acres of garden on the east slope of Shooters Hill—the first and only per-manent home he ever had and where he lived forty years until his death in 1944. It was to be my only permanent home, too, until 1935. The grounds were half-wooded, with bluebells and bracken. There was a detached stable with two rooms upstairs. These gave my father what he had always longed for, a workshop of his own.

Here he installed a large carpenter's bench, a treadle lathe, and his father's tool chest. Later, I was allowed to use the second room as my own workshop and chemical laboratory. It is curious that although these two rooms had clearly been intended for a groom and his family, there were no signs that there had ever been a loo. Seemingly the Victorians had expected their outdoor servants to fertilize the vegetable garden invisibly. There had, of course, never been a bathroom either there or in the house itself. We had one of the three servants' bedrooms made into a bathroom. So while the cook had a room to herself, the two maids had to share. Our loo was a very Victorian affair, entirely enclosed in polished mahogany and devoid of any flushing tank.

Frequently the whole of Shooters Hill would shudder from the shock waves as a great naval gun was tested in the underground proof-butts in the Woolwich marshes. In foggy weather a babble of hooting came from the shipping in the nearby Thames River. I would sometimes visit parts of the arsenal with my father or one of his staff. I watched with awe as the barrel of a fifteen-inch naval gun was turned in an enormous lathe and wound with miles of high-tensile steel tape for greater strength before the final outer casing was shrunk on over it. I was thrilled, too, to watch the giant steam hammer rough-forging a mass of steel that would form the huge breach block. Quite likely that very gun was later fired from the Grand Fleet during the Battle of Jutland.

We acquired a telephone soon after coming to Warren Wood. Our number was 233. It was some years before an extra digit was needed. Dialing was unknown and trunk lines very scarce. Over the years we had many burglaries. The police would be rung and told of suspicious noises. An hour later a nervous detective would arrive on his bicycle ringing his bell like a Chinaman beating his gong to chase the devils away. Nothing was ever recovered.

In the autumn of 1904 I was sent as a boarder to St. Wilfreds at Little Common, Bexhill, a small preparatory school surrounded by wheat fields. Little Common then consisted of just a few isolated houses. We used to bicycle down to the sea and bathe at Cooden, then but an unmanned railway halt with one or two cottages. There was a working windmill on the way to Cooden, and we could see the miller humping sacks of flour or hauling the mill round into the wind with a block and tackle hooked to a big anchor ring. St. Wilfreds was a good little school. Mr. and Mrs. A. E. Clark were conscientious and kind. On Sunday evenings one of the Clarks would read some thrilling tale by Stanley Weynman about Red Indian wars that had happened not so very long before. I became fascinated by maps and designed imaginary countries, using the right conventional symbols, with bridges over rivers and tunnels through mountains. At other times I liked making mechanical drawings of railway points [switches] and crossings, and of goods wagons. One of the two assistant masters at St. Wilfreds introduced me to poetry, mostly in the form of the recently published nonsense book by Hillaire Belloc, with Basil Blackwood's illustrations—a lifelong delight. The teaching must have been quite good for I have no memory of any effort needed to pass the entrance exam for Malvern.

During holidays my mother would drag me away from the workshop to go shopping in Woolwich, Blackheath, or London. Going to London meant a train journey from Arsenal Station to Charing Cross or Cannon Street. In the early days there were horse-drawn hackney carriages and buses. There were hansom cabs, too, with the driver perched high overhead and doors to shut one into a little box underneath. But one walked much greater distances then than now. Sometimes we would take the Tuppenny Tube, Shepherds Bush to Bank for two old pence. It was then so new that people would ride in it just for the experience of traveling through a "pipe." It was the first of its kind in the world. Moreover, the trains necessarily had to be electric, which in itself was a great novelty. The traveling always interested me, but I hated the shopping—except of course at Gamages or Basset-Lowke, the model railway shop.

Around Christmastime Uncle Lexy used to take us to a pantomime. Pantomimes always ended with a "harlequinade," clowns banging about with strings of fat sausages, and tumbling. That was the part I really enjoyed. One such outing sticks in my memory. Uncle Lexy met me at Cannon Street Station to take me somewhere (I forget where). There was a big hole in the pavement from which yellow smoke was pouring, but we walked right into it and down some stairs. I choked and, I suspect, was rather frightened till I saw that people were taking the fumes as a matter of course. Below was a cavernous railway station, with soot-filled air dimly lit by a few naked gas jets. A long coal train rumbled by, its engine belching smoke. I noticed the engine, as a small boy would. It had no cab. The footplate men stood in the open, fully exposed behind the funnel's blast. Presumably a bit of Victorian economic logic—no rain underground, no need for protection. This was the Underground. It had been going in a cut-and-cover tunnel for many years. The original Inner Circle was intended to link up all the main-line termini. Bits of it were still being used for goods traffic. It must have been electrified soon afterward.

In 1904 we bought a motorcar, a Cadillac. Our car number was 443, meaning that it was only the 443d car in the whole of London. The previous year's model is pictured on an ashtray that I still have. Ours was much the same as that picture. It had a single five-inch-diameter cylinder and transverse crankshaft under the driver's seat, Model-T Ford–type gears, and a direct chain drive to the rear wheels. The whole body could be lifted off by unscrewing four bolts. The coachwork still retained much of the curved lines of the horse-drawn age, and there was neither hood nor windscreen; motor coat, cap, and goggles were adequate protection. We knew nothing better. The car was so well designed and built that things seldom went wrong. The main weakness in those early days lay in the tyres. On the one hand, tough synthetic rubber had still to be invented, and on the other, the roads were of water-bound macadam full of sharp crushed flint. My father drove, and on long journeys the family spent most of its time patching inner tubes and plugging gashes in the covers. There were no garages other than a few filling stations since there were too few motor vehicles for roadside repairs to pay. All car owners had to be their own mechanics. Petrol was a very reasonable price. The cheapest was during a price war around 1910 when we paid 11d, or about 5 new pence a gallon.

One summer, I think it was 1906, the Cadillac took us to York-shire and the North Midlands. Between punctures we averaged twenty-five to thirty miles per hour. My father was interested in tracing his ancestors from local records. However, owing to the cha-otic spelling of the name, he failed to go back further than a John Bagnold of Eccleshall, born in 1660. The same person might be baptized with one spelling, married with another, and buried with a third, according to how the local clerk chose to write the spoken name.

Around this time, when I was nine or so, I had what I now be-lieve was almost, if not quite, a unique experience. My father re-ceived an invitation from Louis Brennan for us to come to lunch at their house near Chatham and see his latest brainchild. A rope was lying in big loops about his lawn, and on a straight length of it stood an open model truck, upright and balanced unnaturally without support, like a beached yacht balancing on its keel. The open body, of bright metal, was about four feet long and fifteen inches wide. It contained a twelve-volt battery at one end and a closed box in front. I was bidden to get into it. Being a small boy, there was room for me to sit comfortably. As if alive, it shook itself as I got in, but remained upright. Brennan told me, "I'm going to start it. You will be quite safe. It knows exactly what to do. Just hold on tight to the sides." It ran at a fair speed, straight toward a sharp bend in the rope. Surely it was going too fast and must overturn outward. I held on grimly. But it banked inward, pushing me with it, to just the right balancing angle. The loop completed, it pushed me upright again. I came to an overlapping coil in the rope. The two single-bogies jumped it nimbly, clip-clop, clip-clop. I went on and on, heel-ing over sharply to the right and left as I rounded each bend in the rope. Finally the truck glided securely along a tightrope spanning a hollow in the ground. I switched off the motor and we stopped. Brennan then opened the front box. Two massive flywheels in separate gimbals were spinning in opposite directions at an enormous speed. Their axes were so cunningly linked that their combined gyro effect just neutralized any externally applied torque. He demonstrated this by pressing down on one side with his hand. The two gyros wobbled together, and in doing so pushed his hand back till the truck was again upright.

That extraordinary little truck was never reproduced anywhere, and the idea was never exploited. It was the only genuine monotrack vehicle ever made. H. G. Wells, who referred to it in *The War of the Worlds,* probably saw or heard about it. Poor Brennan. He was a really brilliant designer who worked successfully at an idea but without bothering about its economically practical future.

About that time my father suffered from sciatica. For the next few years he spent most of his annual summer leave taking a cure at Aix-les-Bains, after first planting the family nearby in the foothills of the French Alps. One summer we stayed at Sainte Sixte, another at La Grave in the Dauphin, and another at Argentiere in the Chamonix Valley in full view of the whole Mont Blanc range with its great glaciers streaming down the mountainsides. There was another English family at the Argentiere hotel, with a boy about my age. Every morning before breakfast, father and son would walk along to the snout of the local glacier and bathe in the icy river that flowed from underneath.

My father then began to do five minutes' exercise every morning, and the sciatica disappeared for the rest of his life. Thereafter the highlight of each year for me was the summer holiday on Dartmoor, beginning with the train journey in the Riviera Express on the still-prestigious Great Western Railway. Wonderful on-board lunches with unlimited Devonshire cream were served by soft-spoken west-country waiters. The kind Alger grandparents used to rent for us one of the old moorland mansions that had been taken over from their last owners by the Duchy of Cornwall—Prince Hall, Brent Moor House, or Archerton, the latter six miles from anywhere on the site of a ruined Napoleonic-era gunpowder factory. At Archerton, Enid and I used to catch and saddle our ponies and ride over to Princetown to do the shopping. Dartmoor fascinated me, partly because of its wild, uninhabited expanse and the knowledge of how easily one might get lost or drowned in a bog if the fog set in, as often happened for days on end. Partly too it was the unknown antiquity of the granite avenues, circles, and graves, and the atmosphere of mystery and legend kept alive for me by tales told by Uncle Harold and my grandparents, who had known the moor for generations. Uncle Harold hunted over much of the southern moor. He once mentioned, rather casually, that he had seen three struggling cows sink, one above the other, and disappear into Fox Tor mire before it was drained.

Incidents of that kind most probably created the legends of the "Tom Pearce's grey mare" type, which seem to merge into that of the ghostly whish-hunter occasionally reported to have been heard galloping invisibly over the moor. I actually heard him myself, and it was a very strange experience. It must have been in 1913 or 1914. I was walking with four friends of my own age across the desolate highland of bare black peat and sphagnum moss between Two Bridges and Oakhampton. It had been an unusually dry summer and the peat surface was hard. The sky was cloudless and there was no wind. I began to hear distinctly the sound of galloping hoofs quite close. But there was nothing to be seen. I saw the others looking round, as startled as I was. We all heard it and stopped, wondering. The galloping stopped immediately, but started again, as loud as ever, as we walked on. There is a simple explanation, but as far as I know it has never been tested. By stopping when we stopped, the whish-hunter, I think, gave himself away. The occasion of a dry hard peat surface must be very rare, and on this particular region of the moor, around Cut Hill, the peat has grown, inexplicably, to a thickness of some ninety feet. So it is likely that the whish-hunter was only the sound of our own footfalls echoing back from the granite bedrock far below.

Halfway down the London side of Shooters Hill, near the church, in a large house called Castle Wood, lived Major and Mrs. Charles E. S. Philips. The army rank was uncertain. I think he must have been a Boer War volunteer, though he never referred to it. He had inherited the house and a very comfortable income from his father, the co-founder of Johnson and Philips, the electric cable manufacturers with works at nearby Charlton. Philips was a dilettante in both art and science. He painted in oils (including my portrait, which I still have) and played the violin. He had a droopy-eyed, lugubrious spaniel called Miserable Mernkins. They played ridiculous tricks together.

Philips excited me, as a boy, with the basic idea of science. He instilled in me the urge to discover something more about the nature of things around us by observation and experiment. The start of the twentieth century was an exciting time. Never in the history of the world had so many changes been brought about by so many discoveries and inventions—radio, Xrays, flying, the motorcar, electronics, and, a few years later, nuclear physics and plastics. Charles Philips appreciably influenced my life by stimulating a genuine scientific curiosity beyond my previous interests and expertise in mere workshop mechanics.

Philips had a large and fascinating scientific laboratory, and he always had something new and startling to show me. He once produced an ultraviolet lamp hidden behind a nickel-glass screen which cut out all visible light. In the darkness groups of various crystals fluoresced in unimaginably beautiful colours. He poured what was undoubtedly white paint over my hand and then showed me that it was only a few drops of clear machine oil. He made a heavy iron hoop leap into the air with a powerful electromagnet. Once I found him with no less than three genuine Stradivarius violins that he had borrowed from his friend Hill of the famous little Bond Street shop.

Beside them lay an exact duplicate of a Strad he had made from copper sheeting. There was also an oscillograph and a mechanical gadget he had made for controlled bowing. He was trying to discover what lay behind the magic of the genuine Stradivarius. I helped him with the bowing. He lost interest in the end, I suspect because he realized the impossibility of ever expressing the deadly heresy that to his ear (and certainly to mine) his copper fiddle had just as good a sound.

One room in his lab was devoted to glassblowing. He taught me to make glass ornaments decorated in colour, and how to make various laboratory apparatus. I made a small X-ray tube myself and exhausted it to the high vacuum needed, using a mercury pump I had also made in glass.

Philips became secretary of that venerable place in Albemarle Street, London, The Royal Institution, which still houses the laboratory in which Michael Faraday worked. In spare moments Philips tested X-ray apparatus for hospitals. Although he produced little or nothing in the way of scientific papers, he was a friend of nearly all the leading physicists in the country. I lost touch with him during the First World War; however, in 1921, when I was an undergraduate at Cambridge, out of the blue I got an invitation to tea from the great Sir Ernest Rutherford, then at the height of his fame. That invitation, Rutherford told me, was at the instigation of Charlie Philips.

In 1909, when I was thirteen, I went to Malvern College as a boarder. I never developed any real love for the school, where games were greatly overemphasized. Their organization was, of course, left entirely to the prefects, giving the staff much afternoon leisure. I resented compulsory football and cricket. I was able to avoid both, however, by joining the engineering school where, as an afternoon alternative, I learned to use metalworking tools, lathes, milling and drilling machines, and so on, and techniques such as brazing, case-hardening, and tempering.

We lived in ten houses, fifty or sixty boys to a house. As far as the junior boys were concerned, the social life in a house, especially the fagging, depended largely on the personality of the head boy, and so varied from year to year. It was not good my first and second years, but things improved later. One of my strongest memories of No. 3 House was the winter cold. An ancient greenhouse-type hot pipe ran through the rows of studies, but it was never more than barely warm. My father gave me a room thermometer to hang up, which openly annoyed the house master. The temperature remained in the low forties for weeks on end.

The teaching, done in the classrooms in the college buildings, had three "sides": classical, modern, and army, the latter because the army entrance exam had a syllabus of its own, differing from the university syllabus and, I think, rather broader. It included poetry, European history, and a higher standard in mathematics. I was lucky to have joined the army side. It then had one outstanding teacher, E. C. Bullock. He managed to keep strict discipline with good-humoured laughter which held one's attention and made what he taught so interesting that one wanted to learn more. The math master was good too, in his dry way. He happened to touch off my old interest in maps by casually mentioning that a landscape could be represented by an equation with three variables, so one could devise equations representing mountains, passes, lakes, and rivers. On the whole, I think the teaching on the army side must have been good, for in the spring of 1914 I passed the army entrance exam in fourth place out of several hundred candidates. It was taken for granted that I should follow the family tradition and join the regular army, preferably the Royal Engineers.

After the summer term of 1914, I was as usual on a holiday at Dartmoor with the family. This time, however, it was my last holiday before joining the Royal Military Academy, Woolwich, as a "gentleman cadet." We were staying at the Duchy Hotel, Princetown. Princetown was then a little settlement of warders' cottages, one or two shops, the great prison, and a station at the end of the moorland railway that climbed up through heather and rock to serve the prison. War was declared on the fourth of August. The venerable Aaron Rowe, the hotel proprietor and an old friend of the Alger family, hinted that if we walked to the station at about 10:00 A.M. we might see something interesting. A special two-coach train was waiting there, and presently a small column of men marched in and embarked in military style: reservists, warders, and freed convicts alike, all mixed together. The incident suddenly brought home the meaning of war. Mobilization overrode even the established criminal law.

Because of the war the usual two-year course at Woolwich was reduced to only six months. I can't remember learning anything at "The Shop" that was of subsequent use except a general smartness in mind and body. England had never fought a national war involving vast numbers of conscripts. Military thought was of necessity based largely on the experience of the South African war, then only fourteen years in the past. Mobility was based on horse and mule. Every officer had primarily to be a horseman, so much of our time was spent dressing for and marching to and from the artillery riding school, and doing really strenuous hours of riding. I think I must have become quite good for I was often called out to demonstrate some little feat of equine acrobatics. Indeed, I was in the running for the Saddle Prize but had to drop out owing to a torn riding muscle. Thereafter, as an officer, I hardly ever rode a horse. I could certainly ride as well as most, but curiously we were not taught anything about the horse as an animal, so I was always fearful lest something should go wrong with the machinery and I wouldn't be able to mend it.

In February 1915 I joined the School of Military Engineering at Chatham as a second lieutenant, Royal Engineers. The course here had also been cut down from its normal two years to a few months, but in this short time we learned a great deal that was lastingly useful—how to dig almost effortlessly, how to lift and move great weights with rope and pulleys, a bit of surveying and mapmaking, and how to destroy with explosives. Still more important, we learned to improvise. In addition, as experiences from the current war in France and Belgium filtered through, we were taught how to design, dig, and maintain systems of battle trenches.

One morning while we were out doing fieldwork we saw a mushroom cloud rising from the horizon. This was followed by an intense shock wave. The wind happened to be blowing in our direction, and a little later things began to arrive out of the sky—unwinding rolls of toilet paper, pieces of charts, and wood splinters; then came a naval officer's sleeve with an arm still inside it. Later we learned that a fully laden minelayer, HMS *Bulwark,* in the Medway estuary and about to go to sea, had exploded in one tremendous detonation.

2

France and Flanders
1915–1918

IN 1915, AT the age of nineteen, I was posted as a second lieutenant to the British Expeditionary Force in France. My assignment was with the Eighty-third Field Company, Royal Engineers, of the Twentieth Division. The Twentieth Division had been hurriedly raised as a volunteer formation at the outbreak of war. After training they became a part of Kitchener's army known as "The First Hundred Thousand." They had landed in France only two months earlier. I was sent as a replacement for the company's first officer casualty and was regarded with evident curiosity.

The divisional engineers consisted of three field companies and a signal company. The latter was commanded by Major F. J. M. Stratton, a Cambridge professor of astrophysics who had raised his own territorial unit before the war and brought it out to France. Stratton was later to have a major impact on my life. The three field companies were usually attached to infantry brigades and were composed of four working sections and a headquarters section. The working sections consisted of a selection of carpenters, fitters, draughtsmen, bricklayers, and plumbers. They had a wonderfully comprehensive tool cart. Their main jobs were to supply materials to the infantry and to maintain and lay out new trenches. However, they had many other incidental jobs, including the use of explosives for demolitions.

Army transport in those days was horse- or mule-drawn. The tool cart, for instance, was pulled by a team of six mules with three drivers. In that respect, armies in 1915 had advanced little from the old Roman legions. Vast numbers of animals had to be looked after. Even a small unit such as a field company of Royal Engineers occupied a long stretch of roadway when on the march.

When I arrived, the company was living in a big deserted farmhouse. I was introduced to the officers in the little messroom: the three remaining section officers, Lieutenants Manisty, Schon, and Jarvis; the commanding officer, Major Hopkins; and the second in command, Captain Scott. The latter two were regulars with years of service in India. Hopkins hardly said a word when we were introduced. I soon departed to the room I was to share with Jarvis. Later, I asked him about Hopkins. He replied, "He's the most silent man I've ever met, but he's a damn good CO. After you left he sat there in silence for a long time puffing away at that great pipe of his. Finally Hopkins said, 'He beats you all in boots anyway,' and went silent again." I had been equipped with a beautiful pair of calf-high leather field boots since I was an officer of a mounted corps, trained at Woolwich and Chatham. The boots had been well boned and polished, and as such had drawn the CO's attention. Unfortunately, they were utterly unsuited for trench warfare. But how could the authorities have divined, without any historical precedent, what sort of war this was going to be? I never wore the boots again.

Next morning Scott took me round to see the trench work in progress, the work that I would be taking over. On the way to the front line he told me how lucky the division had been to be sent first to this quiet sector to learn the way of things. Some other divisions had been pushed straight into battle and had never recovered their morale. That walk seemed to me like going across an invisible but active rifle range. Bullets were flying everywhere. In these "quiet sectors" the frontline men on both sides got bored and fired at random, hoping to hit something. Scott took no notice, but when a machine gun started traversing toward us, he fell flat on his face. I quickly followed suit. I had much to learn about the varying probabilities of getting hit by bullets or by the different kinds of artillery shell bursts.

Much of our work was done at night, out in no-man's-land between the opposing trenches. We had to see to the barbed wire or prepare for small infantry raids whose purpose was to capture a few German prisoners in order to identify the enemy's units. Things soon fell into a routine. The routine was broken when, one day, poor young Jarvis was found dead with a stray bullet through his brain. He had left my side only a few minutes before.

Among its assorted implements an engineer field unit carried a load of guncotton for the demolition of railroads, bridges, and so on; so we were looked upon as explosives experts. One day the gunners brought us an unexploded German shell that had landed nearby. It was of a new type and they wanted to see what was inside it. Hopkins, knowing my boyish interest in that line, gingerly rolled it in my direction saying, "Do what you can with the damn thing, short of blowing yourself up." An idea came to me. I tied two one-pound slabs of guncotton—ready primed, fuzed, and electrically wired—each to diametrically opposite sides of the shell. After piling sandbags over it, I blew both charges. I reckoned that if detonated simultaneously, the two inward shock waves should collide and rebound outward. I reckoned too that the unknown explosive inside was unlikely to be detonated by the particular guncotton wave. It worked. I presented the gunners with their shell, split lengthwise into two separate halves, each half containing the original explosive exposed and intact. I had no notion whether or not my little scientific experiment had already been done. Probably not. Anyhow, that small incident is the first example I can remember of my "try-it-and-see" attitude to problems.

Later in 1915 our division was sent north to the Ypres Salient where fighting was almost continuous. We became part of a special new corps, the Fourteenth, together with the Guards Division and the

Sixth Division, which was one of the regular British formations. The Fourteenth's commander was Lieutenant General the Earl of Cavan, a professional soldier and the former successful commander of the Guards Division.

The Ypres Salient formed the extreme left of the long Allied trench line that stretched across France to the Swiss border. Farther north lay low, marshy sea flats intersected by dykes. Through this ran the sea-level Yser Canal, north to the coast from the cathedral town of Ypres, which had been devastated by bombardments. The Germans had hoped that by capturing the Ypres Salient they might outflank and perhaps roll up the Allied line. Attack followed attack, first with chlorine gas and then with liquid fire. All were repulsed, though with heavy casualties. The front ran in an arc around the east of Ypres, along a low ridge which ended at the canal. Here the last British trench abutted on the German trenches that continued northward along the eastern canal bank. The western bank had been held peacefully by a French division of elderly reservists; that low country was quite unfit for operations.

Our division was to hold the extreme northern end of the Allied front where it ended at the Yser Canal. Each unit sent an advance party to reconnoiter. We found that we were to relieve men of an unlucky and dispirited division. The trenches were in ruins from previous bombardments and reached by rickety wood walkways across the stale and filthy water of the hundred-foot-wide canal. All movement in the Ypres Salient was by night, for the Germans over-overlooked everything from higher ground. As we had half expected, the Germans attacked in the darkness on the night of the actual takeover. There was heavy shell fire and some confusion, but our fresh troops held on and quickly dug themselves in. The job of my little section had been to maintain the canal bridges in a usable condition between bursts of machine-gun fire from the Germans farther along the canal bank. The division had done well, for the takeover had not been easy. A note of personal praise came from our corps commander, Cavan.

A month later we moved to the east of the salient, to better, higher ground. The area was littered with corpses from previous battles. Attack had been followed by counterattack for months, passing over the same no-man's-land between the opposing trenches, in places only a few yards wide.

On one occasion, a particular German machine gun had become a serious nuisance. I was told to destroy it with a newly thought-up gadget called a Bangalor Torpedo. It consisted of a set of metre-long tubes filled with explosives that could be fitted one into another and pushed forward over the ground. With a blackened face I crawled out toward the enemy line, pushing the torpedo ahead toward the German gunner. Its nose hit something and stuck. I wriggled alongside the torpedo and found the nose buried in an old corpse, not ten feet from the German gunner. I could see the gunner's face and waited until he turned around, then quickly freed the torpedo and pushed it closer to the German. I wriggled backward slowly, luckily escaping the machine gunner's notice. Back behind our lines, I thrust down the exploder handle. The machine gun was gone. I never wanted to do that again.

The entrance to one deep dugout was labeled "177 Tunneling Co. RE." I sometimes went down to see the owner, a Danish mining engineer named Dalgas. He had a strong German accent that often got him arrested. Dalgas ran a grisly underground war of his own. His galleries ran out across no-man's-land, and his sappers listened for work going on in similar enemy galleries. They would hear digging for long periods, followed by tramping with heavy loads toward our lines. It takes some time to transport and lay a thousand tons of TNT in a confined space. When the carrying stopped, Dalgas would have a small charge blown at the end of our gallery to block off the German gallery, killing those in it like wasps in a nest. Sometime later he would break through and acquire the Germans' TNT. Earlier on, the Germans had blown a giant mine, obliterating a whole battalion; but nothing like that happened after Dalgas developed his countermeasure. South of us, the British blew a mine with four thousand tons of TNT—four kilotons in nuclear terms.

In the spring of 1916 we were living in cellars in Ypres, working all night up front and trudging back at dawn across the causeway over the old moat to the Menin Gate through the medieval ramparts. There was always some poison gas around from German shells. Sometimes we had to don our clumsy masks, but usually we just coughed our way through. Our cellar was home. Up its stone steps we looked across wrecked public gardens to the skeleton of the cathedral, whose tower was a favorite German target. The buildings around had been reduced to rubble. Nearby ran the main artery through the town, often a shambles of mangled six-mule teams after a direct hit. A rosebush stood in stark contrast at the top of our steps. It bloomed before we left.

One morning, alone in our cellar, I was awakened by descending footsteps. At the entrance stood a dapper man wearing a red and gold–braided capband and gold-braided red tabs. To my astonishment it was Lord Cavan himself, the corps commander. He had come to check on things in person and to make himself known.

The output of artillery and ammunition from England was ever increasing. In addition to field guns, there were much heavier weapons like the 9.2-inch howitzers, a replica of which now stands at Hyde Park Corner in London as the Artillery War Memorial. In the offensives of 1916 and after, guns of all calibres were crowded closer than axle to axle. A bombardment generated a fearful din. Once while on leave at my parents' home in Kent, I became aware of a faint pulsation, continuous but irregular. It was not an audible sound, more an endless succession of thumps. The ground shocks originated in the thudding of those big howitzers. It was our bombardment of the German lines over in France before a major offensive. It went on for six days.

In July 1916 Cavan's Fourteenth Corps marched south to the Somme country. The great offensive that was to end the war had started on July first. The attack on the northernmost sector had been a complete and ghastly failure, with an enormous loss of life. Near the end of the month the Twentieth Division was put into the line in the Hebuterne region as a temporary stopgap. The front there had previously been exceptionally quiet, and buildings and green fields were relatively close behind; however, pieces of bodies were everywhere. Buried bodies squelched underfoot as one walked. The ill-fated Thirty-first Division had planned to attack "over the top," but they never got the chance. The Germans had known the precise hour and minute of the attack, no doubt from their listening sets, and they concentrated all their artillery on the trenches, burying the occupants. When we arrived a month later, thousands of bodies still lay where they had fallen. The sandy soil, loosened by the rain, had collapsed to fill what remained of the shattered trenches. Green-backed flies swarmed over them under a blazing sun.

A few days after our arrival there was heavy shelling and I took cover in a large shell hole. It was raining hard. The head and torso of a man slid quietly down beside me. There was nothing below the waist.

Early in September 1916 the corps moved to the rear of the southern sector where the offensive had been more successful. One day a rumour spread that something very strange was to be seen nearby. In a big field, groups were talking together excitedly, as people do when confronted by something new and unexpected. There were lines of weird machines, their crews busy around them—the first "tanks" ever seen had reached the front. They had been a well-kept secret. I think that I am right in saying that no track vehicle of any sort had previously been made. Yet the idea was logical enough. The bigger the wheel, the better it rides over rough ground; consider the "penny-farthing" bicycle. But it is not the wheel but a small slice of tread that touches the ground, so why not cut away the rest of the wheel and short-circuit the tread back on itself?

The first tanks were crude and clumsy things, more like reptiles than like modern tanks. Guns were mounted in barbettes projecting from each side like great eyes. Lacking a differential drive, steering was done by the sideways movement of a big tail attachment that stuck out behind. However, those first tanks were the forerunners of a revolution in warfare.

Next day we were moved up and learned that we were to attack together with the Guards Division on our left. There followed the usual terrific bombardment by our massed artillery to soften the enemy. Our division did well in the ensuing battle. We captured two villages, Guillemont and Guinchy, and pushed out beyond into the beginning of the green countryside. Guillemont had disappeared in the bombardment, save for a brick or so and a few bits of splintered timber sticking out of the earth. But there was no breakthrough. The artillery bombardment had left the land torn up, cratered, and roadless, and this prevented transport by wheel or hoof from supporting any continued advance. After firing a few shells and causing initial consternation among the Germans, the tanks had also got bogged down. Five divisions of cavalry had been standing by to exploit the breakthrough, but they remained idle. Cavalry was never again to be used.

The war was slogged out for another two years. The bit of green land we had seen soon turned brown and died. The shelling continued. There were new faces everywhere. Few of my old friends from a year ago had survived.

At the end of 1916 I was transferred to the signal branch of the engineers, owing to the machinations of my father, himself an old signals man, now understandably an anxious parent. With the outbreak of war, Father had been recalled from retirement. He was given an interesting job as one of a small team of technical troubleshooters helping industrial firms through the early stages of taking over the manufacture of munitions, which had previously been made by the government in Woolwich Arsenal. Later he became director of an embryonic research and development station which expanded to include a satellite station at Biggin Hill.

During 1917 I worked with the Fourteenth Corps signals. The then Prince of Wales, afterward the uncrowned King Edward VIII, had a staff captain's job under Cavan. He often joined our signal officers' mess. Being only twenty-one like myself, he seemed to find our mess more congenial than the general's "A" mess to which he belonged. We were a bit sorry for that frustrated and rather irresponsible young man. He longed to go to the front and take an active part in the war, but was firmly restrained by Cavan for fear he might be taken prisoner. He resented being treated, as he thought, like a small boy. He was a charming young man with a permanent chip on his shoulder.

I finally got my wish to join the Nineteenth Corps signals under Stratton, my old Twentieth Division friend. Stratton was now a lieutenant colonel and responsible for all the corps communications. The Nineteenth Corps was in the Ypres Salient, about to take part in the great Passchendaele battle. The whole scene in the salient had changed. Ypres was no longer overlooked by the Germans. New railway lines had been laid, and light tramways had begun to bridge most of the impassable crater desert. Military communications have never been so complex, before or since. In the back areas there was hardly a field without a route of forty to a hundred telephone lines running through it on hop poles. Lines ran in vast networks between this centre and that, little huts or dugouts where parties of linemen worked day and night at great terminal boards. They checked, tested, and changed wires as one after another route was cut by shell fire. The complexity continued in the forward areas. Overhead wires were replaced by great bundles of multicore cables buried deep in the ground. Cables ran from signal dugout to signal dugout, each of which was in turn connected to scores of gun batteries, infantry brigades, dressing stations, ammunition dumps, and sound-ranging stations.

Complicated and ever-changing records were kept at corps headquarters, but Stratton seemed to have in his head the routing of every line of the vast system. Each day some arterial route would be cut, and always a short jet of soft, barely audible orders quickly came from this astonishing little Cambridge professor of astronomy, providing an alternative communications route. Even on the eve of the big battle, when the bombardment had cut most of the main lines and when many of the linemen had been killed by mustard gas, Stratton remained calm. His plans for an elaborate makeshift were developed in a minute, without looking at any records.

Never have I seen or heard anything like that initial bombardment before the Passchendaele offensive. The corps's front extended only two thousand yards. But in that distance there were 1,600 guns of all calibres: 18 pounders, 6-, 8-, 9.2-, and 12-inch guns, and even 15-inch howitzers. They spread out row after row in an endless array. They were nearly all behind us, firing over our heads and facing the mouth of our dugout. Each gun was firing every few seconds into the darkness. Dancing tongues of green and red fire spouted from the ground. The din was beyond description.

Over to the east, on the main Passchendaele ridge, whole villages were blown up, woods disappeared, and the courses of streams were changed. Yet the isolated teams of German machine gunners, immured in ferroconcrete pillboxes, survived the bombardment and caused huge casualties in our advancing infantry.

I took over the work on a new, deeply buried cable line at the front. It was very like the old days with the Eighty-third Field Company. Big working parties had to be organized. There were no mechanical diggers in those days, of course. Nearly all the work was done at night. Some nights it was impossible to work through the gas shelling. Later on, in the autumn of 1917, the craters filled with water, turning the ground into a quagmire in which many men drowned. Presently there came a false spring, and a green slime spread over the soggy, dead land.

I stayed with the Nineteenth Corps signals until the end of the war. We continued to rely entirely on cable communication. Radio, then called the "wireless," was still in its infancy and very primitive. It was used only in cases of extreme emergency, for the good reason that the science of cryptography was then elementary and all messages were liable to interception. Speech by radio was a thing of the future.

Communication through buried cables was effective for semi-static warfare. However, the system broke down entirely during the long and rapid strategic retreat of Gough's Fifth Army in the final Battle of Amiens in 1918. For five days army headquarters lost all touch with its corps commanders and seemed to us to have disappeared. The corps commanders also lost contact with their divisions. Our own headquarters was moving back once or twice a day. Stratton managed not only to maintain contact with our divisions but collected all the other lost divisional headquarters in the Fifth Army. On the morning of the fifth day of the battle I was occupying the middle compartment of a three-door canvas loo when the corps commander, General Watts himself, entered the neighboring loo while his chief staff officer settled on the other side. Not knowing I was there, they continued their conversation. The chief of staff said, "I can't understand that little man. I'm told Stratton has had no sleep for four nights, yet he's as chirpy as ever and has a better-detailed grasp of what's happening than I have. He knows just where everybody is and has everything at his fingertips." "Yes," said Watts. "If he had chosen to be a soldier instead of an astronomer, he'd have made a better commander than any of us. But I wish he wouldn't talk quite so fast. At least he does repeat everything twice."

The Armistice on 11 November 1918 came as a stunning shock. The ties of comradeship that had held us together, that had bound the individuals of the great army into one enormous machine, were gone. The machine had suddenly become purposeless. The unifying objective had disappeared. Of the million or so British servicemen in France, half had experienced no other kind of adult life. The long delays of demobilization led to increased impatience and anger. Little incipient mutinies occurred in many units. There was no trouble under Stratton. That active, chubby little man exuded cheerful common sense. He kept us all too happily busy to grumble.

It became clear to the authorities in London that there were too many young professional officers for peacetime needs. In early 1919

Stratton showed me a new Army Council instruction allowing any young regular officer who was sufficiently qualified to spend two years at a university. There would be no pay, so it was a form of extended leave. Stratton suggested that I follow him to Gonville and Caius College, Cambridge. I jumped at the idea. What better way could there be of investing my war savings?

3

Cambridge
1919–1921

I RETURNED TO England in March 1919 and was temporarily posted
to the War Office in London as a junior member of the signals
directorate. I was to remain there for the five months until I was
due to go to Cambridge in the autumn. It took me most of that time
to learn the long-established governmental system of dealing with
documents in the Central Registry and Branch Memos. I got to
know who should see what and what to do when a "green label"
file arrived, a file containing parliamentary questions that would
have to be answered at once by the minister.

I lived at home at Warren Wood and commuted by train to Charing Cross. In my lunch hour I was able to do some shopping for my
mother. Nobody told me never to use the imposing Whitehall entrance or the grand staircase within, but I did wonder vaguely why
I saw no one but very senior generals. I finally realized my impudence when, as I was mounting the stairs carrying a parcel of fish,
the minister himself—Winston Churchill—raised a rebuking eye-
brow as he passed.

I went to Caius College in October as a freshman. There I discovered that Stratton, now Professor Stratton, was to be my "tutor."
A tutor does little or no teaching. His role is to act *in loco parentis*

toward the undergraduates under his supervision, to watch over their lives and offer help in any private trouble.

The year 1919 must have been an anxious one for the university authorities. Almost empty during the war, the university was faced with a sudden flood of freshmen with war experience who were up to four years older than usual. When a friend of mine was chided by the dean for failing to attend college chapel, he responded, "But my dear dean, I've just come from Germany where I commanded a town of thirty thousand inhabitants. There will have to be some compromise about this." "Indeed there will," said the dean, "but it will all turn out right." So it did, and without impairing any of the ancient traditions of the college. There were naturally a few miscalculations. For example, 1919 was the year of the Einstein Eclipse, and Professor Eddington, the leading exponent of relativity at Cambridge, was billed to give an open lecture. Based on previous experience it was estimated that fewer than a hundred people would be interested in such an abstruse subject, and accordingly a small lecture room was provided. Virtually the whole university turned out. The venue was switched to the Great Hall of Trinity College, but even then half of those who came had to be turned away.

The new students had a dangerous capacity for spontaneous combustion. Through someone's misjudgement a notorious pacifist demagogue was allowed to hold an open meeting. A great crowd collected and a riot ensued. The lecturer, pursued by the crowd, barely escaped to his host's private house, which was surrounded by a walled garden. Someone called "One, two, three," and a hundred yards of stone wall fell flat. The students then dispersed quietly, having expressed their dislike of the lecturer.

The master and fellows of Caius coped effectively with that sort of contingency. Realizing that collective steam had sometimes to be let off, they had the foresight to arrange for Stratton to be in charge of those ex-servicemen who were most likely to be restless. Now and then he would subtly suggest to us the possibility of some relatively inoffensive but spectacular and amusing student rag. So we freely confided our plans to him, and he in turn often suggested improvements.

Among the rags in which I took part was the affair of the "Jesus gun," worth mentioning because of its odd sequel. Caius College had accepted, as a war memorial, the offer of a surplus field howitzer. By a clever trick of relabelling, the gun was delivered to Jesus College instead. There it was quickly mounted on a concrete platform to which its wheels were securely bolted. The apparent theft rankled us. My close friend Hoppy Hopkinson conceived a plan to retrieve the gun late at night for its rightful owners. Nothing was left to chance. Volunteers spent several nights on the Jesus College grounds cutting through the steel bolts with hacksaws. A gun party with dragropes was needed to wheel the gun through street-lit Cambridge. Duplicate keys had to be made for our own college gates and the hinges oiled. Decoy parties of sprinters were also needed to lure away any police or proctors who might be around. The operation went off without a hitch. At daylight the gun stood in Caius College behind locked gates, without any evidence of how it got there.

That year Hoppy decided on an army career and applied as a university entrant. He was refused because he was two months over the age limit. Stratton thereupon sent the War Office a copy of Hoppy's operation orders for the gun affair, with a diplomatic letter saying in effect, "This is the chap whose application you turned down on grounds of being two months over the age limit you had chosen." Hoppy was duly accepted as an officer cadet. Eighteen years later, Major General G. F. Hopkinson was commanding an experimental airborne division when he was killed.

I took engineering as my degree subject. I soon found that the Cambridge engineering tripos course was too theoretical to be of much use to me. I worked reasonably hard, however, and finally got a fairly good honours degree. There was such a crowd of freshmen that first postwar year that the ex-service majority were expected to take their degrees in two years instead of the customary three. Extra teachers had to be brought in to cope with our numbers. The instructor who taught us differential equations was particularly good. He made the math amusing and easy to remember by choosing symbols so that the equations spelt out rude words or statements. Unfortunately, his style became cramped when a solitary girl joined the course. (Miss Chitty afterward became a world authority on the safe design of great storage dams.)

I did not take the degree course too seriously. I wanted instead to acquire as wide an outlook as possible and at the same time to recover something of the lost three years of my youth—to make the most of the free irresponsibility of undergraduate life. I sometimes crept into lectures on other subjects taught by the great authorities of the time. This was more to get the atmosphere than to understand the lecture. I heard Sir Ernest Rutherford's booming voice at the Cavendish Laboratory, talking about the structure of matter. I listened to Sir Joseph Larmor, one of the leading mathematicians of the age. I missed John Maynard Keynes's lectures, if he gave any, but often saw him on the street, a satanic figure with huge black eyebrows who had dominated the Versailles peace conference.

It may have been the elementary teaching of history at Malvern that stimulated me to obtain a still wider knowledge of world history. Why should history as then taught in schools be confined to the glorification of the British Empire? What had gone on elsewhere, over the whole of Asia and the Middle East? The great university library was handy. As a relaxation from engineering I read Howorth's *History of the Mongols,* in four volumes which told about their vast Asiatic empire, their catastrophic invasion of Europe only seven hundred years earlier, their three-hundred-year domination of Russia, and their destruction of the Arab empire of the caliphs. That naturally led to Muir's *Life of Muhammad,* the great conquests of his immediate successors, and their impact on Mediterranean Europe and the Crusades. I then wanted to know something of still earlier empires—Persia, Rome, and ancient Egypt—and to link events to a common time scale. H. G. Wells had the same idea a few years later and wrote *The History of the World* with his son Gip.

One's friendships may be classified according to the degree of intimacy, as a random distribution spreading indefinitely from a small nucleus of close companions to ever-widening circles of lesser interest which contain a host of casual acquaintances. Among the engineers, my little nucleus included G. F. Hopkinson, who later became a general and commanded our first airborne division; Cedric Outhwaite, a wartime naval lieutenant and son of an obstreperous politician whom he resembled; and my roommate Alfred Harvey. Also there was Tommy Kirkpatrick, an entomologist taking an agricultural course. Tommy was the irreverent son of The Very Reverend Dean of Ely. He had been an observer in the RFC during the war and was badly wounded when his pilot was killed. Then there was Maurice Eyres, one-eyed from an injury in the war, taking modern languages at Cambridge. Among the medical students were Bill Copeman, son of a Harley Street specialist and later himself to become a Harley Street specialist in rheumatism, and one Dobie, who some years later became our kind and much-liked family doctor. I had not kept in touch with the boys at Malvern (the majority of them had been killed); however, the friends I made at Cambridge were different. That little nucleus remained close for years afterward, though all are now dead.

We never ceased to wonder at the smooth efficiency of the college machinery—the result, I suppose, of six hundred years of experience by a carefully selected body of dons. We usually dined in hall, several hundred of us. Two excellent dinners were served each day. In less than twenty minutes after the opening Latin grace we had all eaten and unhurriedly departed, leaving the high table to dawdle on. The bed-maker, an elderly lady who had been with the college for a very long time, did all the daily jobs from cleaning the rooms to doing laundry and mending. College rooms had no running water, so she also brought hot water in the morning. I could stroll into the buttery and order a dinner for six or ten on only an hour's notice. This would be served in my rooms, so boys would arrive bringing tables, chairs, and drinks. Then three courses of a first-class dinner would in turn be carried in on covered trays. In due course, all would be removed. The cost might run to half a crown a head, twelve pence in today's money.

We also wondered at the prodigious and almost sleepless activity of Chubby Stratton. It was customary for the tutors to invite two or three students to breakfast in their rooms. Some of us breakfasted often with Stratton. He was always brightly alive, yet those who had occasion to cross the court to the loo during the night had never seen his lights out before 4:00 A.M. He told me once that he never needed more than three and a half hours of sleep. On top of his administrative work, his tutorial and teaching tasks, and his nightly sessions at the observatory, he had taken on the heavy job as secretary to the International Astronomical Union, intent on pulling it together again after the war. Yet he was always available when wanted, always ready to help and to jot down another job to be done that day on his already crowded schedule.

During vacations, and on occasion in later years, a small party of three or four of us would go off on some unconventional trip abroad, usually to a lesser-known region in France. We traveled cheaply, preferring good food, drink, and peasant hospitality to the greater comforts of commercially minded towns. On our first, and now most memorable, trip, Hopkinson, Tommy Kirkpatrick, his brother, and I bought an open flat-bottom raft in Orleans that had been used for carrying river gravel. It was relatively small and barely held the four of us. We floated lazily down the Loire, making only enough effort to keep steerage around the many sandbanks. The Loire flows through the Anjou wine country, past a succession of great medieval chateaux, each of which we visited. It is a broad and uncontrolled river, usually very shallow but liable to sudden violent floods, and the French considered it unnavigable. The locals were incredulous that we had arrived by water on a small boat. Each night we tied up below some little hamlet, trusting to find an inn of some sort. We enjoyed the simple village food. The patron would produce bottles of his own homegrown wine. Then a farmer or two would join us and chat idly. Eying the bottles, someone would say with a wink at the patron, "Why are you drinking that muck? Try some of mine. It's far better." This went on until we staggered to a bed of straw for the night.

We passed through Tours, where we were arrested on a misunderstanding, and on to Angers, our final destination. After tying up we were joined by a pleasant young man, the son of the manager of the Cointreau factory. He escorted us on a tour around the factory, where we watched and smelt the elixir being poured by the gallon from a big tap. We were each given a bottle. The trip had come to an end, so we sold the raft, for more money than it had cost us.

There were other trips—to the Vosges with the Kirkpatrick brothers, Bill Copeman, and two medical students, and to the Pyrenees. A walking trip in the strange Causses country in southwestern France took us through an almost barren limestone plateau carpeted with nothing but wild lavender. The plateau was intersected by the thousand-foot-deep gorges of the Tarn and the Lot rivers. The weathering of the rock walls in these gorges had left clusters of hanging pillars resembling ogres' castles. The people in the narrow sunless villages along the Tarn seemed to have a circulating economy by which they lived on trout and crayfish that in turn fattened on the effluents from the people upriver. Those gorge villages were so narrow, and the upper floors so overhanging, that one could reach across and touch the window opposite. Once we were awakened near midnight by a soft noise across the street. A man was quietly finishing off a coffin by the light of one candle. We were reminded that long ago these people had been decent Christian heretics, the burned victims of the Albigensian Crusade, whom legend later came to accuse of ancient sorceries.

4

Ireland
1921–1923

I RETURNED TO the army in the summer of 1921 and was posted to Ireland. There I joined the Fifth Division Signal Company stationed at the Curragh, the long-established army centre in County Kildare. After the 1916 rebellion Ireland had been virtually under military rule. With the end of the war in Europe, the garrison was reorganized to consist of three of the six peacetime divisions, responsible respectively for the south, centre, and north of the island. The Fifth Division, with its headquarters at the Curragh, was responsible for the central region, from Dublin to the west coast.

The army was greatly helped in keeping some semblance of law and order by the notorious Black-and-Tans, a semimilitary force whose tough, unorthodox methods were highly effective. They consisted mainly of restless ex-conscripts who had failed to readapt to peacetime life. In 1921 the British government had already begun to realize the hopelessness of continuing its repression of an alien, irrational-minded race who had an innate sense of separate nationality stemming from a vague legendary past. Home rule for the whole island had been found impossible owing to the intransigence of the Protestant north. The only rational alternative was to grant some sort of self-rule to the Catholic south. The difficulty there was to find a sufficiently strong group to negotiate with, and at the same time to persuade the British public that it was necessary to deal with men whom they had come to regard as assassins. Ultimately, quiet discussions with a moderate group of rebels, led by Michael Collins, showed some promise of settlement in the form of an Irish Free State. But it was clear that Collins would have an uphill job to hold authority over the republican extremists.

Meanwhile, a partial truce had been tacitly accepted, although a few of our troops were still being murdered by extremists and country houses were still being burned. The situation in the Catholic south was complicated by the biracial origins of the people. The "O's," mostly the primitive, smallish, dark stock of unknown origin, were taken to plotting great deeds while hanging about street corners. They were mixed with the English settlers from Cromwellian and later times, landlords great and small in big old-fashioned manors trying to keep an English outlook with a brogue. If they were reputed to "take no part in politics," their houses were liable to be burned, so their attitude was rather unreliable.

I arrived during this transition period. My job involved much travel by car, the railway being out of action due to destroyed bridges. I had to cross the Bog of Allen from the Wicklow Hills in the east to Galway and Sligo in the west, with Athlone in the centre, to look after the wireless stations which linked the outlying army detachments. The roads were then still passable, although one had to approach the ubiquitous humpback bridges with care because many had had their crowns blow away, leaving a wide, invisible gap. Some reckless young officers killed themselves trying to jump a broken bridge by driving at high speed, although a few did manage to land safely on the far side. There was a vague feeling among us that the air in Ireland must be making everyone a little mad, including ourselves. It seemed mad, for instance, to insist that every officer must at all times keep an automatic pistol in his pocket, cocked, in spite of the number of accidents it caused. At fancy dress dances at the Curragh Club, the GOC would stalk in and accost some unfortunate young officer, "Where is your pistol?" He was only obeying orders issued from Dublin.

A smelly old he-goat roamed over the open Curragh, the traditional racecourse of Ireland. He also wandered into various adjoining gardens. The colonel took a keen interest in the mess garden and became exasperated by the goat's ravages. One day he could stand it no longer and cried, with Henry II, "Will no one rid me of this turbulent goat?" Immediately four young officers leapt out the window and shot the goat at point-blank range. Some days later three of us were sitting on the front seat of a bus in Dublin. (We were allowed in Dublin provided we wore civilian clothes and always kept one hand in our gun pocket for safety.) We happened to be recalling the incident aloud, naturally referring to the goat as "he." On glancing around, we noticed that everyone had quietly slipped away.

On one of my trips across the Bog of Allen I stopped for a night at the little hotel in Castlebar. At another dining table sat four dark men with black hair covering the whole of their faces, nose and all. I asked the old waiter in a whisper who such men could be. He whispered back, "They are mountainy men. They come here sometimes." Neanderthal might have better described them. Later in the meal I remembered that I had forgotten to bring my razor, so I borrowed an old-fashioned naked one from the waiter. I stupidly thought, "Now he's less likely to cut my throat."

Michael Collins finally signed the treaty with the British government, and the army began to leave the south. However, it remained doubtful whether the new Free State army would be strong enough to hold their own against the Republicans. In our area they were hesitant to take over the Curragh for fear of being attacked, and only agreed after the GOC promised to leave them the big searchlight tower whose great eye had for so long roamed over the countryside at night and awed the inhabitants.

After leaving the Curragh, many of the troops were temporarily housed in gaols. Gaols make quite practical makeshift barracks since they have cooking facilities. Our company lived first in Mary-borough Gaol (now Port Laoishe, Ireland's top security gaol), and then at Carlow. Never having lived in gaol before, we were naturally interested in exploring. We investigated the hanging shed, a separate brick building of two small rooms. I was standing looking up at the gallows beam when someone pulled the lever. I dropped six feet onto a heap of lime.

The treaty allowed for a continuing British presence in the extreme southwest as essential for our naval defense of the western approaches. It was agreed that the two great harbours of Cork and Bantry Bay should remain under our direct control, and this was accomplished, respectively, by our occupation of the fortified islands of Spike and Bere. I was posted to these islands as OC Signals Western Approaches, together with a small signal detachment and a subaltern. I therefore left the Fifth Division Signal Company before they returned to England. We had been a happy unit. The commanding officer, Major R. E. Barker, was experienced, kind, and efficient, and had become a good friend. Originally an Australian stock farmer in the outback, he had joined the ANZAC corps and first served in the Gallipoli campaign. He then transferred to the British army and ended the war as a political agent among the independent tribal chieftains in Kurdistan, where he acquired some lurid stories. He taught us how to crack a twenty-four-foot stock whip without killing each other or ourselves. Once he confidently took me into a Dublin slum to watch an illegal badger-baiting session. Eighteen years later in Egypt, General Barker was once again my commanding officer.

With the murder of Michael Collins, civil war broke out all over southern Ireland between the 'Staters and the wilder Republicans. There was a strong republican element in County Cork, led by a mad half-Russian lady with the grand old Irish name of Countess Markowitz. The lovely country around Bantry Bay was full of "wild mountainy men." Synge's "Playboys of the Western World" were fighting amongst themselves. From the aloof isolation of Spike Island in Cork Harbour we heard the rattle of machine guns and the boom of artillery. At night we watched the intermittent glow of the flames of burning houses on the mainland.

Our tiny islands were armed with permanent coastal-defense artillery manned by garrison gunners, a static lot. Apart from them, the only other British were the crews of three V-class destroyers on somewhat carefree detachment from their base at Devonport. Other than these three destroyers, we had no communication with the outside world. Irrespective of the weather, they brought our mail, pay, and food on round trips from England. The Irish mainland was out-of-bounds. All but local movement on the mainland was dead, for virtually every road and railway bridge had been destroyed.

There was little for us to do on our isolated outpost. Finding the garrison gunner officers dull company, I made friends with the navy personnel, in particular with the officers of HMS *Velox*; her skipper was Lieutenant Commander Tovey. I had a dinghy with an outboard motor and was able to help with transport for little parties aboard or ashore. I sailed in *Velox* as a passenger along the coast, to and from Bere Island, and sometimes on much longer Atlantic patrols. We were supposed to keep out of sight of land, but now and then a headland would appear on the eastern horizon. Each time that happened we would see a column of smoke—the natives had lit a warning beacon. On one trip Tovey had orders to call at a certain disused lighthouse, presumably to contact a spy. Number One started ashore in the motorboat but was fired on from the lighthouse and had to turn back. Bullets hit *Velox,* penetrating her thin quarter-inch plate and wounding one of the crew. This was such an insult that Tovey retaliated with his four-inch gun, destroying the lighthouse.

During one patrol we ran into bad weather. In port a destroyer seems quite a large ship, but in an Atlantic storm it can be thrown about like a leaf. The freeboard was only four feet. *Velox* would climb slowly up a great wave, dither on its crest, and plunge down to half bury herself under the next oncoming wave. To make the risky journey from cabin to wardroom, one had to crawl along the open deck in oilskins, clinging hand over hand to a steel rope. I found things much too exciting to think of seasickness.

One day, out in the Atlantic, Tovey had a birthday. To celebrate the occasion, the ship's armament was exercised. Depth charges were ejected, the four-inch gun was fired, and machine guns were trained on basking sharks. Years later, Admiral Tovey was our naval commander in chief during the Second World War, responsible for the desperate operations ending with the sinking of the *Bismarck*.

I returned to England in 1923. Army Signals had just been transferred from the Royal Engineers to a new Royal Corps of Signals. I was posted to the new signal training centre at Maresfield Park in Sussex, first as instructor of electricity, and later as chief instructor at the School of Signals.

Since the whole of Ireland was still nominally part of the United Kingdom, service there was counted as home service. As a result, I soon became due for foreign service.

5

Egypt
1926–1929

I ARRIVED IN Egypt in the autumn of 1926 in a troopship, together with my Morris two-seater and a year-old Alsatian dog called Cubby. I joined the signal company which formed part of that anomalous army establishment known as the "British Troops in Egypt." The status of these troops in a foreign country needs some explanation. Since the Middle Ages Egypt had been a province of the great Ottoman (Turkish) Empire, which included the Balkans, Syria, Mesopotamia, Palestine, Arabia, the Sudan, and Libya. With the gradual decay of the central government, the outlying provinces became increasingly independent. The Balkans broke away, and Libya was ceded to Italy in 1904. The rest remained nominally subject to the sultan, who by tradition was the Defender of Islam.

Egypt was governed by a khedive, or viceroy, and the vast Sudan, until the dervish revolt in 1884, had been an Egyptian colony misgoverned with scandalous corruption. With the pacification of the Sudan after the Battle of Omdurman, the country became a "condominium," nominally ruled jointly by Britain and Egypt but in reality a British protectorate to whose budget Egypt contributed a small sum for the privilege of flying its flag.

At the start of the nineteenth century, an Albanian bandit named Mahamet Ali made himself khedive and founded a dynasty which lasted until the end of the First World War. Since there was no longer a Turkish sultan, the khediviate became an independent kingdom under King Fuad. The nobility remained largely Turko-Albanian and the system of government remained Turkish, while the native villagers, or fellahin, products of some six thousand years of first-cousin marriages, remained unchangeable.

The construction of the Suez Canal by Khedive Ismael Pasha and the lavish cost of the opening ceremonies ran the country into a huge foreign debt, mainly to Britain and France. Payment of the debt required an intolerable taxation which, together with gross misgovernment and corruption, led to the Arabi rebellion in 1882. The security of the debt then became so uncertain that the London government was forced to support the khedive with a military force. A strong strategic reason for this drastic step lay in the need to secure the canal as a vital link in our trade route to India and the Far East. With the British troops came that political genius Sir Evelyn Baring, of the great banking family, with instructions to minimize local resentment at the virtual occupation of the country. Adopting the selfsame policy as the Roman emperor Augustus, Baring effaced himself under the lowly title of British agent. Leaving the government system apparently intact, he appointed carefully chosen advisers to each department. In this way, while the dignity of Egyptian officialdom was maintained, he became the éminence grise and later, as Lord Cromer, the real master of the country, backed only by the peaceful and friendly presence of a small military force. Such was Cromer's brilliant diplomacy that, in spite of successive British governments' vacillating policies, he was left in charge for the extraordinary period of twenty-four years to carry through the gradual reforms by which he became known as the founder of modern Egypt. The British troops in Egypt became an almost traditional institution.

During the First World War the small British force was vastly increased. Egypt became the base for all our operations against the Turks. But the BTE, short for the noncommittal name British Troops in Egypt, shrank again to its former peacetime size when the war ended. There being then no foreseeable external threat to the country, the BTE's role reverted to that of internal security, that is, protection of the Egyptian government in case of riot or rebellion. There was only one change. Since by the Versailles Treaty all the mandated territories were governed by high commissioners, and since the Egyptian khedive was now a king, the former low-key Cromer policy had to be abandoned and the British representative also became high commissioner. The incumbent at the time of my arrival in 1926 was the very lively and capable Lord Lloyd, formerly head of the wartime Arab Bureau which had kept an eye on Lawrence's doings in Arabia. His main job now was to see that internal politics did not get out of hand.

The peacetime role of the armed services involved both training in readiness for the likely future war and a lot of administration. A part of the signals' job was accomplished in liaison with the Mediterranean Fleet. Our periodic meetings were usually attended by the fleet signal officer, a tall, immaculately dressed, and rather distant lieutenant named Mountbatten.

Peacetime soldiering leaves a lot of leisure time. Egypt fascinated me from the start, just as Dartmoor had done when I was a boy. Both had the strange aura induced by the physical presence of the remote past and also great, bare, trackless expanses where the careless might well get lost. Just as one could step out from the edge of Princetown onto the open moor, so here one could cross the last irrigation canal into a desert of rock and sand that stretched westward, unbroken for a thousand miles.

The unmarried officers of the engineers, signals, and tank corps lived in a combined mess in Abbassia Barracks on the eastern desert outskirts of Cairo. Except for two of us, the inmates were all young postwar officers. Most spent their leisure time at the Gesira Sporting Club, where every kind of recreation was available. A few others of us, bitten by the country, its people, and its past, wandered further afield, to the huge five-thousand-year-old cemetery of Saqqara near ancient Memphis, with its elaborate tombs, or to the great depression of the Fayyum, below sea level and watered from the Nile by a canal dug four millennia ago and still in use.

At that time exciting discoveries were being made, most relating to the earlier of the thirty-three successive dynasties of ancient Egypt. The anniversary temple of the third-dynasty pharaoh Zozer was being uncovered for the first time. Not only did it show the highest standard of stonemasonry ever attained, but the fluted columns, long believed to have been the invention of the classical Greeks, showed that the style originated two thousand years earlier. The flutes were found to be an exact imitation in stone of the current pillars of Nile mud cast in vertical fascines of palm branches held together by cords. Even the knots in the cords were faithfully carved in limestone.

I watched the lion body of the Great Sphinx being slowly exposed from the sand that had buried it. For ages only the giant head had projected above the sand. As of old, gangs of workmen in continuous streams carried sand away in wicker baskets on their heads, supervised by the traditional taskmaster with the traditional whip, while the appointed song leader maintained the rhythm of movement. When at last the great forepaws were exposed, there stood between them a neat tablet proclaiming that Pharaoh Thutmose IV of the seventeenth dynasty had had the curiosity to have the same thing done three thousand years before. Even in his time, it seems, the thing was a mysterious relic from some bygone age. It is now believed that the Great Sphinx is a portrait memorial of the fourth-dynasty pharaoh Khafre, who reigned a generation later than Zozer and was the immediate successor of Khufu, who built the Great Pyramid. Khafre himself built the second largest pyramid alongside and just behind the Sphinx.

During the reign of Zozer there lived an extraordinary man named Imhotep, seemingly Zozer's vizier, who became the legendary father of writing, medicine, and philosophy. He was known to the classical Greeks as Hermes Trimagistos. As building in stone appears to have been developed in Zozer's time with the first idea of a pyramid, it is possible that Imhotep was also the innovator of stonework and of recording in stone.

The genius of those old third- and fourth-dynasty people is astonishing. Khufu's Great Pyramid involved quarrying, transporting, and lifting two and a half million blocks of limestone averaging between two and three tons in weight. Inside, a massive sarcophagus of polished granite weighing many tons was levered up the grand staircase to the tomb chamber. The original smooth outer casing of the pyramid was stripped off by Saladin in crusader times to build the Citadel of Cairo, leaving a series of over a hundred steps, each about four feet high. In connection with a project to hold a military tattoo, I had occasion to calculate the seating capacity of one face of Khufu's pyramid. An idea of the tremendous size of the structure can be gotten from the fact that one face could comfortably seat twenty thousand people. Owing to the annual Nile flood, the whole population in the old days must have lived on the desert banks for three months each year with nothing to do. It has been suggested that the outburst of pyramid building between the third and sixth dynasties may have been a practical means of solving a serious unemployment problem, as well, perhaps, as mere royal ostentation.

We visited and climbed all forty or so lesser pyramids and read all that was known of their histories from Professor Breasted's recently published book. The old man was still working in his mud house near the Giza pyramids, and he was a delight to talk with.

I was intrigued as well by the complex modern irrigation system, with its combination of canals and lower-level drains, and by the age-old wooden machinery still in use for lifting water from the Nile onto the fields. The unchanging peasant people too, in their mud villages among the date palms, were another source of wonder. In spite of a 1,300-year-old veneer of Islam, a ceremony was still held in Upper Egypt in which the ancient gods were carried in procession from one ruined temple to another. Near Cairo the start of the Nile flood is celebrated each year by "The Cutting of the Khalig" in which the east bank of the river is breached to let the water flow toward the Red Sea through a canal dug by the great engineer pharaoh Amenemhat III in the twelfth dynasty, four thousand years ago. The original ceremony has persisted.

It soon became clear to me that my little Morris car was quite unsuitable either for the rough mud roads of the Nile Valley or for the stony going along the desert edge. Captain Victor Holland, an officer of my own age and a schoolfellow at Malvern, owned a Model-T Ford that seemed able to go anywhere. It even climbed the old rock stairway up the Mokattam cliffs to the citadel. I bought one like it and a new horizon opened for me. My wanderings no longer had to be confined to the Nile Valley. There was so much of the ancient East to be seen in Sinai, Palestine, and Transjordan—relics that few had been able to see because of the absence of roads and the lack of time for camel travel across country. However, there were two snags to be overcome. First, there were no roads out of Egypt, so help would be unavailable en route in case of breakdown. We would not only have to be as self-contained as possible but would have to travel with more than one car. Second, neither the Egyptian Frontier Administration (FDA) nor the Palestine police would allow casual desert trippers to wander about at will because of the unnecessary bother of having to rescue them in case they broke down or got lost or stranded. So we had to learn just what our Fords were capable of, and we also had to convince the authorities that we were responsible enough to stay out of trouble.

An early trial trip followed the old caravan road from Cairo to Suez across barren, waterless desert. This nineteenth-century road had been built by a naval engineer as part of the overland route to India, but it was abandoned after the Suez Canal was opened. The distance was only fifty miles and the road had been so massively built that it might have carried heavy modern traffic, but the journey took us a whole day. The building contract had evidently omitted to include provision for culverts to carry off storm water. Whole sections had been washed away, soling, boulders, and all. We passed the ruins of a waterless palace built to the orders of a former mad khedive. We also passed the ruins of the caravansery where my grandmother must have spent a night during her journey to India.

On that and a number of other short trips into the eastern desert, up dry, trackless wadi beds into the Red Sea hills, we learned a great deal about what the cars could and could not do, and about their petrol consumption over various types of going. We developed a simple camping routine, in the open without any tent. I soon got to know the officers of the Egyptian FDA, and in particular Major Jarvis, the governor of Sinai. Pleased that anyone should take an interest in his manor, he allowed us to cross the canal (there was one ferry station) and go anywhere we could get our cars to. The bedouin would report our movements via Jarvis's tiny posts of Sudanese policemen. It was easy to get ten days' leave from army duties. In those short periods we made several pioneering car journeys in Sinai and beyond, into Palestine and what was then Transjordan.

We traveled to the famous monastery of Saint Katharine and spent a week there with the monks. After we were ferried across the canal near Suez, we followed a rough track along the west shore of the peninsula for some ninety miles, and then turned east into the mountains up the stony bed of the Wadi Feiran. Some way up, the narrow valley opened to form a tiny rock-walled oasis. Beside it rose the precipitous six-thousand-foot mass of Mount Serbal, all of bare red granite. This was the traditional Mountain of the Lawgiving. As though Serbal itself was not impressive enough, every one of the scree of large boulders below it was scrawled over with the bold symbols of some archaic writing. The picture, at least to the Semitic giant-addicted imagination, was complete, broken tablets and all. This mysterious Sinaitic writing is thought now to be nothing more than an ancient collection of "wasms," or tribal marks.

The little oasis of Feiran must at one time have held a small religious community. But in the sixth century the Christian emperor Justinian visited the place. Whether because of the squalor he found or because of its defenselessness, he closed it down and had the present fortress-monastery built thirty miles farther up the valley. Strangely, all the traditional Mosaic associations—the site of the burning bush, the cleft where Jethro hid, and so on—were also moved up the valley.

For good measure, we were snowed upon that night with manna, not from heaven but from the tamarix thicket under which we slept. It seems as though that same strain of tamarix must have been growing there in Moses' time. The manna, a faintly sweet form of sugar of no food value, comes from an exudation caused by an insect.

The Greek church-monastery is indeed a fortress. Until the previous century it had no ground-level entrance. Everything was hoisted up by rope. Standing five thousand feet above the sea, surrounded by granite peaks, it has remained a Christian island in a Moslem ocean. Even the savagery of the Arab conquests passed it by. Though laden with the rich gifts of centuries, it has never been plundered.

Each of us was given an adequate little cell, and our attention was at first occupied with the hospitality of the monks and their Old World courtesy in tending to our every need and showing us round the monastery. So it was not till we had attended a service in the chapel that I began to feel a sense of an enormous continuity with the antique. Nowhere else in the world could the feeling be so strong. The same prayers in the same Greek language had been chanted in the same chapel without a break for fourteen hundred years. The monks themselves were still living with half their minds in the Byzantine era. The clock kept Byzantine time, the hours starting at 6:00 A.M. Prayers were chanted for blessings on the emperor and his officers of state. Some special festival took place that Sunday. The abbot, who still held the Byzantine title of archbishop of all Sinai, wore a magnificent robe laden with jewels and gold. Later, I watched the robe being folded most carefully and stored away in a coffer of solid silver whose lid needed two monks to lift. I asked the robe's history. "That particular robe," they said, "was presented to us by our gracious Empress Irene." According to Gibbon, she lived in the eighth century.

We were introduced to Brother Thomas, custodian of the mortuary. It seems he had died, robed and sitting in his chair, a century or so ago, and he had been left there to desiccate in the high, dry air of the place. There he sat, upright, overlooking his desiccated brethren. The monks were evidently fond of the old fellow, cheerily stroking his chin as they passed. His head nodded gently. There was nothing repellent in the fresh air of that tidy chamber. Indeed, there seemed to be a peaceful continuity with the obvious struggle for existence in the living monastery.

When we reluctantly left, the abbot refused to accept any compensation for our keep. The Order forbade it.

On another occasion we made an ambitious journey to visit ancient Petra, in the new kingdom of Transjordan, by an untried southern route via Aqaba at the head of the eastern branch of the Red Sea. The still-turbulent tribal kingdom on the highlands east of the Dead Sea was then barely eight years old. The security chief, an Englishman named Peake Pasha, had raised a police force capable of keeping a reasonable degree of order. Peake had kindly agreed to look after us in the volatile Petra region.

Between Egyptian-owned Sinai and Transjordan lay the broad, low-lying valley of the Arabah, the southern extension of the great rift from the Dead Sea to the Gulf of Aqaba, a no-man's-land across which there were no known tracks. Having crossed the plateau of northern Sinai without difficulty, we were faced with the problem of getting our cars down the two-thousand-foot escarpment to the bottom of the Arabah. There had once been a way cut in the rock by an Egyptian army a century before, but unused since. Jarvis had

1. Map of the eastern Sahara, Sinai, and Palestine showing the expedition routes of 1927, 1928, 1929, and 1930. The 1928 route to Bir Terfawi was a locust-control expedition that Bagnold guided. They discovered the Selima Sand Sheet in 1930.

told us we might possibly get down, but certainly not back up again. We crawled down very cautiously, the whole party manhandling the cars one by one as they skidded with ominous rumblings of loose stones on outward-sloping hairpin bends. Often the gradient was one-in-three, with a precipice outside. We got down, but Jarvis was right in saying we had no chance of getting back by that route.

At the bottom we found the plain of the Arabah to be a sticky saltmarsh, virtually impossible to plough through. We seemed to be stranded. The sea of the Gulf of Aqaba was quite close, however; there could be no sticky salt crystals on its bed. We tried driving with the car wheels submerged about half a foot. Yes, there was good firm sand beneath. We managed to travel like that right across the head of the gulf to the little village of Aqaba.

Aqaba, the country's only future seaport, was then isolated from the rest of the kingdom by a five-thousand-foot escarpment. The village had but one old, partially collapsed wooden jetty, on which a decade earlier supplies had been landed for Emir Faisal and T. E. Lawrence during the Arab revolt against the Turks.

Peake had passed word of our coming. We were welcomed by a burly Negro policeman, formerly a Turkish official, treated hospitably to a large Arab meal, and given the police station for the night.

Next day we had the escarpment to climb, up the long, stony, winding bed of the Wadi Ithm, and then up a succession of steep, sandy passes. It was a severe test for our old Model-Ts, but we made it, laboriously, to the sudden civilization of the little town of Maan. There were even shops where petrol and food could be bought. A train was standing at the terminus of the former Hedjaz Railway, which used to run on precariously to Medina, protected by Turkish troops.

The remains of Petra lie in a naturally eroded pit surrounded by vertical pink sandstone walls. The place is not far below the crest of the great escarpment that lay to the north of our ascent. I doubt it could ever have been a city in the sense of a living place. It is too small and too full of altars, high places, and stairways leading up to elaborate tombs, all cut from the solid rock. It was probably the

Nabateans' sanctuary. They were a trading people who had establishments along the west coast of Arabia. My chief impressions of Petra were its startling state of natural preservation and the even more startling modernity of the strange architectural style. Some of the tomb façades might well have been designed last century instead of two thousand years ago.

Approaching the entrance to Petra, we were confronted by a menacing group of fully armed tribesmen on horseback, no doubt intending to rob us, just as their fathers had robbed Charles Doughty in Victorian times and just as Burckhardt had been robbed a generation before. However, at that moment there came another clatter of hoofs. Peake's police had arrived, led by a knowledgeable Druze officer who spoke good English and was to become our guide and friend. Later, he mentioned the existence at and around Petra of an odd tribe of seemingly non-Arab starvelings who sheltered among the ancient tombs. He sent two police to catch one for us to see. A wretched scarecrow in a tattered garment was brought in. We were told that the local Arabs looked on them as hardly human.

The return journey north to Amman, thence down and across the Jordan, through Palestine—then a British mandate—and across Sinai was hurried and uneventful.

Later, we made another journey in the same region, this time along the little-known hundred-mile length of the Arabah rift, from Aqaba northward down to the Dead Sea, fourteen hundred feet below sea level. Peake lent us an armed Arab policeman as escort, for that no-man's-land was likely to harbour many refugees from justice, and probably drug traffickers as well. We saw no one, though, for they hid at the sound of cars. We passed far beneath the site of Petra, away up in the eastern escarpment, and also beneath the dome of Mount Hor, where some forgotten sect still zealously guarded the tomb of Aaron with rifles. In biblical times that high eastern escarpment would have been seen from Jerusalem, frowning across the rift and cursed many times as Moab and Edom, the home of evil men who raided the opposite Judean hills.

At last the long, winding descent along a dry watercourse, deeply incised below the valley floor, came to an end. An evil-smelling swamp occupied the whole valley, which was densely covered by reeds well over head height. The heat was intense, the humid Dead Sea air stagnant and oppressive. Yet there were men living down there. We heard them calling to one another and caught a glimpse of two strange figures. Our police escort, increasingly nervous, insisted that we quit that dismal place.

Peake told me later that he had once gone down there in an attempt to learn who those people were. All he got, he said, was an incoherent story that they had once lived in a city that was destroyed by fire. They had pointed to a hill shown on the map as Jebel Usdom, which with the common Arabic transposition of the first syllable becomes Sodom.

> A land of old upheaval from the abyss
> Where fragments of forgotten peoples dwelt.
> (Alfred Lord Tennyson, *Le Morte d'Arthur*)

The story is doubtful, however, for it may have been implanted by some missionary in the recent past, if indeed any missionary is likely to have ventured down to such a forsaken place. There is of course plenty of salt about for Lot's wife. It has been mined at the southern end of the Dead Sea for at least three millennia. Now, the Israelis have driven a highroad all along the western shore of the Dead Sea and on to the Red Sea. The fragments of forgotten peoples are no more.

The planning and success of these expeditions had been such fun and had given us such confidence in ourselves that I determined to attempt an exploration of the still largely unknown west, into

> Desolate horizons where
> The desert terrible and bare
> Interminably rolls.
> (Hilaire Belloc, *The Modern Traveller*)

About this time the huge and costly expeditions of the past, of Scott and Shackleton to the Antarctic and the early Everest expeditions, were giving place to much smaller and vastly cheaper journeys by small groups of young men undertaken at their own expense and with next to no backup, using novel methods of overcoming natural obstacles. Geno Watkins, with a tiny party, was exploring for the first time the great Greenland icecap, and Eric Shipton was climbing remote and unscaled Himalayan peaks.

In Cairo we had at our very doorstep the edge of a vast field for real exploration. The eastern Sahara, or Libyan Desert, stretched westward from the Nile for a thousand miles, the most arid region on Earth, waterless and lifeless save for a few artesian oases scattered several hundred miles apart. To the ancient Egyptians it was the land of the hereafter, ruled over by Osiris. Herodotus reported the loss of a Persian army that was overwhelmed and buried in a sandstorm. Since then many people have lost themselves and died of thirst. A great wind-erosion desert has a frightening lack of continuity; no ever-downward valleys, nothing but isolated hills, plateaus, and depressions, with no distinct landmarks visible from afar. Vast areas remained unexplored.

The Libyan Desert had never been crossed in its entirety in the east-west direction because of a biological barrier—the limited endurance of the camel with neither water nor grazing. This barrier had been pushed farther west by the enterprise of Prince Kemal el Din, but only at the enormous expense of a large-scale expedition equipped in regal style and transported in a fleet of semi-track vehicles. He made two outstanding journeys into the unknown at about the southern latitude of the Sudan border. He told me emphatically that one thing he had learned on those long journeys was that mechanical transport could never cross the ranges of sand dunes that lay as barriers across the desert floor. He had tried, as had others before him, to penetrate westward from the Egyptian oases farther north, but the huge dune ranges of the Great Sand Sea, of unknown extent, formed in his opinion an insuperable obstacle.

This struck me as an irresistible challenge. Could our light cars possibly do what the prince's heavy caterpillars could not? I began making tentative plans.

Just then, however, I became due for promotion to major. There being no vacancy for a major in Egypt, I was to be transferred to India for the remainder of my overseas tour. I was to join a certain troopship and had packed all my belongings in readiness. Then, out of the blue, came a message from BTE that my passage had been postponed. The Egyptian government had urgently asked that I might be allowed to help them by acting as navigator of an expedition their Ministry of Agriculture was sending to an isolated patch of vegetation far to the south, near the Sudan border, to cope with a possible locust invasion. The spot lay somewhere in a vast, utterly featureless sand sheet, and none of their own people knew how to get there. I had recently designed and made a pilot model of a sun compass that would avoid the awkwardness and unreliability of a magnetic compass when jolted about on a cross-country journey. The great Selima Sand Sheet was indeed featureless. Moreover, a general mirage brought the sky down to within a hundred yards in front of us. We saw distant chains of dunes as yellow airships floating in the sky. Guiding our party blindly, the sun compass led us accurately to the map position we aimed at. There was the water hole just ahead of us. I felt quite a thrill at realizing that abstract calculations about the sun could apply so truly in real life. The locusts had disappeared after eating all the surrounding vegetation. We searched a wide area, but they had gone with the wind.

Thereafter I duly sailed to India (then undivided, India comprised the whole peninsula). However, the lure of the unknown parts of the Libyan Desert was still very strong. In odd moments I continued to plan an expedition into the Great Sand Sea. Early in 1929 Imperial Airways started the first commercial service between England and India. That same spring, taking a short period of leave, I flew to Cairo, as almost the first paying passenger, to finalize things with the other five members of the projected party, all of whom were officers still serving in Egypt. We had planned to start that autumn when the weather would have begun to cool. By army tradition, exercises were also confined to the same cool period.

A new general was then commanding BTE. I discovered to my annoyance that he had refused to give them leave. Pharaoh would not let his people go. So, like Moses, I decided to appeal to God, in the person of the chief of the Imperial General Staff in London. I forget how the interview was arranged, and I am unsure how I could have had the cheek, but I flew on to London and saw the chief himself, surrounded by several generals, and explained the position. I was not then serving in BTE, and so was not going behind anyone's back. He was friendly enough and promised, in effect, to tell the BTE commander not to be so rigidly military. The experience we would gain might even be useful. He kept his promise. Pharaoh let his people go.

Early that autumn, along with two friends who were going on their annual home leave, I drove a Ford truck from India to Egypt. We crossed the Baluchistan desert just south of the Afghan border—more or less across country—before reaching Persia, then traveled a thousand miles across that country through Meshed, Teheran, along the ancient Royal Road of Darius and past his famous rock inscription at Behistun, across the Syrian desert to Damascus, and finally through Palestine and Sinai.

In Egypt I joined the rest of the party. We drove another 150 miles westward across country to the outer rampart of the Sand Sea, a continuous forbidding wall a hundred feet or more in height. It took us some days to discover the general character and strange, almost lifelike, organization of this sand landscape. The dunes were unlike anything Prince Kemal el Din could have seen elsewhere. They were far older and on a much grander scale. Each of the endless, unbroken ranges, all parallel to one another, was to our astonishment so firm that our car wheels did not sink in. But the general appearance had clearly misled the prince. Each range was overlain by comparatively shorter ranges of high, steep, and utterly uncrossable dunes. These, but ten miles or so in length, overlapped each other, leaving a narrow lane a few yards wide of firm going. These lanes, imperceptible from a distance, had been overlooked by the prince. We could with care drive up and through the lanes. The edges of the firm strips were invisible, though, and if we happened to override an edge, the car was liable to tip suddenly forward, axle-deep into a dry quicksand.

Lack of time prevented us from going far. The weather had been against us, too. A storm blew up. A dense, stinging fog of low-flying sand grains wholly obscured not only our cars but ourselves up to our shoulders, while our heads stuck out against a clear blue sky. One after the other, our feet dropped an inch as sand was scoured from beneath. The whole landscape was on the move. We had to keep the cars moving, blindly. Luckily the storm was brief. But worse trouble followed when one car broke a half-shaft. We had to return to Cairo for a replacement, two hundred miles of rocky going. Returning forty-eight hours later, we found the car on its side at the bottom of a wind-scoured crater eight feet deep. The feeling grew that these huge dunes were alive, that they resented our intrusion and were warning us of what they could do if they chose. We had learned, though, that one dune range was exactly like the next, and that the Great Sand Sea was no longer inviolate.

The following year, 1930, we penetrated more than fifty miles west into the great sands without seeing any solid ground—nothing but curving dune crests to the horizon. The going was getting progressively easier. We had to turn south, though, hoping to trace the extent of the sands in that direction, and were obliged to follow a lane between two chains of uncrossable high dunes. After some two hundred miles, there happened what we had all silently feared. The two dune chains flanking us closed together into a jumble of soft sand into which the cars sank axle-deep. Strangely, we did nothing. We lay down content on the scorching sand, numb to bodily discomfort. The dunes had got us, but no matter. Had we remained in that state, we should undoubtedly have perished. It was Douglas Newbold who diagnosed what was wrong. We had unknowingly got badly dehydrated. We broke into the water ration and drank a pint each. It had the effect of a strong whisky and soda. We jumped up, got the cars extricated, and turned round. Ten miles back to the north, we spotted a little passage through the eastern wall of dunes that we had previously passed unnoticed. We had escaped.

It was on that 1930 expedition that we first grasped the extent of the great Selima Sand Sheet, a corner of which I had seen two years earlier. Driving eastward from Uweinat to the Nile, we crossed the whole three hundred miles of it. A single utterly flat sheet of firm sand, it is now known to cover an area of nearly 100,000 square miles. Driving at speed for hour after hour, on a compass bearing, often blindly into a mirage, it became hard to stay awake. On one occasion both occupants of a car did fall asleep, the driver's foot remaining hard down on the pedal. They were only retrieved after an anxious chase.

Only two objects broke that vast monotony—a solitary little projecting rock but a foot high and a single, isolated barchan dune. We camped in the lee side of the dune, leaving our rubbish to be buried beneath its sand. Fifty years later, that little heap of rubbish was found in the open by geologist Vance Haynes. The massive dune had passed over it and was then a quarter of a mile or more downwind, making the rate of march 24.6 feet a year.

We had learned a great deal about how to exist and travel, self-contained, over long distances. We replaced the Model-Ts with the improved Model-As, which had bigger tyres, and also replaced the touring-car bodies with simple wooden pickups which gave much more cargo space. Our unit of packing was the eight-gallon wooden petrol case holding two four-gallon disposable petrol cans. Each case measured eighteen inches by eleven and was fourteen inches high. We had the box bodies made an exact number of cases wide and long, so there was no tumbling about or wasted space. These wooden cases could hold either petrol, water, or food. The water was carried in empty petrol cans supplied to us by the Shell Company of Egypt. We filled them with water and soldered the lids on. I have drunk water from cans that had been hidden in a cave for seven years.

We had established three strict rules: (1) never travel with only one vehicle beyond walking distance from help; (2) never leave anyone alone out of sight of a landmark that is not clearly visible from far away; (3) never use water for any other purpose than drinking or topping up car cooling systems. Cooling water was conserved by leading the radiator overflow through a pipe to the bottom of a two-gallon can set beside the driver. The can was half full of water so that any steam would condense in it. Ultimately, if the can became full, a jet of boiling water would force the driver to stop. He would have been warned by feeling the connecting pipe getting hot. Having turned into the wind and stopped the engine, a loud gurgling sound would be heard in less than a minute—a vacuum had drawn the water back, leaving the radiator full to the top.

Every unnecessary item was discarded in order to get the maximum payload of supplies. In a rainless country there is no need for mudguards, windscreen, or engine cover. For ourselves, we carried nothing but our bedrolls. Loose sand made the best possible bed under the stars. We carried no cooking gear other than one round cook pot eight inches in diameter and about the same depth. This pot had two handles which supported it in a square four-gallon can from which we had cut the top and the lower half of one side. Fuel from the wood case was fed in below. Unopened canned foods (with paper labels removed) were boiled in our tea water. One case of fuel was more than enough for the six of us.

An imperative need had long been a quick and practical method of extricating a vehicle sunk axle-deep in soft sand and unable to move. Earlier, for our trips in northern Sinai, we had looked for some kind of ramp to get our Model-Ts up or down little vertical-sided water runnels. In a Cairo junk shop we found a few steel channel sections, five feet long and about eleven inches wide, which had been intended for roofing dugouts during the First World War. We found them to be the perfect answer to the sand problem. A little valley was scooped out by hand from in front of each rear wheel, sloping downward to the base of each tyre. A channel section was laid in each valley, on which the wheels could bite as the car accelerated forward. This usually carried the car well beyond the front ends of the channels, and, we hoped, onto firm sand. The car's two occupants, working together, could complete the operation in a very short time. A decade later, most army vehicles were similarly equipped.

Another vital need was an ability to navigate surely and accurately while bumping over rough ground, sometimes having to hold on with both hands. It was essential to remove any lurking fear of getting lost. My sun compass played a large part in the system we evolved. Simply, it was a steel knitting needle set vertically in the centre of a horizontal white shadow disc three inches in diameter. The face of the disc was graduated in 360 degrees of bearing, and the disc could be rotated in its fixed mounting to follow the sun through the day from east through south to west, according to a card giving the sun's azimuth every ten minutes of the day. Since solar time was being used, the card also gave the equation of time for the calendar day. The compass was mounted on the dashboard of a car and was always exposed since our cars had neither windscreen or roof. The sun's shadow was always visible, even when the sky was overcast. Occasionally, around midday when the sun happened to be directly overhead, there was no shadow. But this caused no trouble because it was the period of our midday meal. The great advantages of a sun compass are that it is deadbeat, shows true bearings, and is independent of changes in the positions of magnetically uncertain spare parts carried in the vehicle. Leaving the driver to pick his own way, and holding nothing but a pencil and notebook, the navigator concentrated on recording mileage and bearing. At every halt, out came the map, protractor, and latitude-longitude scale, and the last bit of course was plotted. In the evening the dead-reckoning map position was checked against the astrofix position calculated from readings taken with theodolite, chronometer, and time signals. The day's plot was rarely more than 1 percent off, even when the route had involved much wriggling between hills and sand dunes.

We needed to carry a number of map sheets, however blank they might be in this unknown land. An army formation carried a three-ton truckload of maps, each tightly rolled. Finding a particular map was difficult and time-consuming, and when found, a sheet had to be unrolled, perhaps in a strong wind, and weighted flat with stones. We needed something much less cumbersome. I made a plywood case the size of an Egyptian 1:500,000 map sheet folded in half. All our maps were kept flat and secure, and the thin case occupied little space.

I wore sandals, the only type of shoe from which sand could be kicked out freely, and a felt hat with big gaps cut from the sides to ensure good ventilation and to avoid cooking my head. The one nuisance we never thought to find an answer to was sand blast on the side of one's face in a strong wind. We took this to be inevitable.

Usually our parties consisted of six men in three Ford cars. When fully loaded, each car had an entirely self-contained range of fourteen hundred cross-country miles. How tough and fit we were in those long-ago days. To load the cars we would throw eighty-pound eight-gallon petrol cases to one another in a chain. To keep fit during the hot summer months, I took fifteen- to twenty-mile walks along the top of the Mokattam cliffs, scrambling down the rocky sides of successive wadis and up again. Those summer months were the season for our annual two-month home leave. Travel was by ship and overland, and I usually stopped off for two or three weeks in the Alps. The first week was taken up in getting acclimatized to the altitude after the flatness of Egypt. Then I began climbing, in rather a hurry. One year I climbed two fourteen-thousand-foot mountains, Monte Rosa and the Matterhorn, with only one day's rest at Zermatt in between.

Of the many friends I made in Egypt, I might introduce here those who will reappear later. Douglas Newbold, a big man in all senses, a few years later became the political head of the Sudan government. He seemed to know every tribe in that huge country, and their customs and special needs. He was an Arabic scholar with a deep knowledge of the country's history and literature. He had a great sense of fun and was an acquisition to the 1930 expedition. Bill Shaw, just as practical, had the precise scientific mind for accurate detail. He took over the nightly job of position-finding from the stars by theodolite, time signals, and laborious calculations. Years later, during the war, he was my obvious choice for the post of intelligence officer.

Guy Prendergast, a captain in the Royal Tank Corps, took part in most of our trips from the beginning. He was a versatile young man who could both fly and mend a light aircraft as skillfully as he could repair a car or tank. Especially helpful friends were the British staff of the Egyptian Desert Survey, headed by Dr. John Ball, a geologist by profession, whom I regard as the father of Egyptian exploration. Barely five feet tall and almost totally deaf, he had traveled with the Light Car Patrols during the First World War and had guided Prince Kemal el Din on both his great expeditions. He gave me much encouragement and sound advice. His assistant, and soon his successor, George Murray, and George's wife Edith, became close and lasting friends. It was they who introduced me to the pleasures of mountaineering. Their hobby in Egypt was the exploration of the Red Sea hills to discover the quarries whence the ancients had got the stone for their jewelry and statuary. George had a vast knowledge of Egyptology and also of the modern people, both the valley bedouin and the unchanging peasants. Assuming as he did that the native mentality could not have changed much, he made the ancient doings seem real and natural. He also had an inexhaustible stock of fascinating stories.

The Egyptian Desert Survey had two expert cartographer-surveyors, Pat Clayton and Dennis Walpole. We occasionally came across one or other of them way out in the desert with a single Ford truck, one little tent, and one or two trained bedouin. We once rescued Walpole from an awkward situation when he was stranded through loss of engine oil. I got to know Pat Clayton well. He was an Irishman with prematurely grey hair and an active, inquiring mind. He was a really first-class craftsman—no office draughtsmen for him. He produced the final master map sheets himself in his little tent, perfect lettering and all.

6

India
1928–1931

IN 1928 I sailed to India from Port Said, Egypt. My young Alsatian, Cubby, followed solo in the next troopship, since there was no accommodation for a dog in mine. He evidently had a wonderful time in the charge of the ship's butcher, for he arrived full of bounce.

Most of that year was spent at the signals depot at Jubbulpore in Central Provinces, learning about the Indian ways of life. In November of the same year I moved to the Northwest Frontier Province as OC Waziristan District Signal Company. The nature of that peculiar province needs some explanation. The only natural physical frontier of the Indian peninsula in the west is the great Indus River. The fertile riverine land stretches out west of the river in a narrow strip. Beyond this strip the laws of India ceased to operate. Farther west, the wild, mountainous country merges with Afghanistan and was occupied by independent Pathan tribes who had lived for centuries mainly by raiding the Indian plains. Neither the previous Mogul nor the British governments had been able to curb this raiding or to reach any binding frontier agreement with Afghanistan. Successive British envoys dispatched to Kabul had either been repulsed or murdered like my grandfather's friend Alexander Burns. Successive punitive expeditions had achieved nothing, and many lives had been lost. In 1901 the viceroy, Lord Curzon, introduced a new "forward policy." He unilaterally proclaimed a frontier, known as the Durand Line, well inside tribal territory and stationed permanent garrisons there to restrain the tribesmen. A new Northwest Frontier Province was created, embracing the whole region west of the Indus. This was divided into districts according to traditional tribal boundaries. The southernmost of these was Waziristan, inhabited mainly by the Wazir and Mahsud tribes.

The district was governed in part by a civil Resident, assisted by British political officers fluent in the Pushtu language who wore tribal clothes and moved freely among the people. The Resident shared the task of governing the district with the major general who commanded the mainly irregular troops stationed in a few strongly defended forts. The district headquarters were at Razmak, which had become a small military town. Razmak lay six thousand feet up in the Suleymen Mountains and was reached by a long, winding mountain road. I had been warned that by tacit agreement with the tribesmen, the Razmak road was sacrosanct by day, but anyone using it after dark was fair game. While waiting to be shown my quarters in an officers' mess when I arrived in Razmak, I noticed a posted note from the Resident: "The Tori Khel have offered in part atonement for shooting my political officer, a gift of four sheep. I have accepted this and will be glad if your mess will take one." British-Indian law certainly did not apply here!

I was accompanied to Razmak by my bearer, Shafiullah, and my Alsatian, Cubby. A good bearer is one of the blessings of life in India. He acts as valet and housekeeper; he engages, rules, and pays one's servants and foresees every household need; he acts as courier when one travels. Shafiullah was loyal, conscientious, and scrupulously honest. He was a Moslem. I had been warned at Jubbulpore, and previously in Egypt, not to employ a Christian servant as they were in general untrustworthy. I had a curious example of this when I once motored home from Egypt with Tommy Kirkpatrick through Palestine, Syria, Turkey, and the Balkans. Tommy had acquired a set of wheel chains for his car. They were difficult to get in Africa, and he treasured them. They were kept in a box on his running board, where they were handy when needed. Neither of us gave much thought to them until we crossed the Bosphorus into Europe. Approaching Adrianople, I spotted the first church and commented, "We're entering Christian country, hadn't you better lock up those chains?" Brought up in a cathedral atmosphere, Tommy just laughed. We stayed the night at a hotel. Sure enough, next morning the chains were gone.

Since the mutiny in the previous century, all units of the Indian army were composed of mixed races or religions, with each contingent under its own Viceroy's Commission officers. My unit was composed of Madrassis, Punjabi mussulmans, and Sikhs. The Madrassis are a very different race from the northerners, completely black but definitely non-Negro. They are probably descended from an aboriginal race driven south long ago by the invading Aryans. They proved to be quick and intelligent. My senior Indian officer was a wise old Sikh. Any of the British (King's Commission) officers was senior to any Indian officer. This two-tier structure was necessary and had worked well. The Indian officers were content with their status, realizing their comparatively limited outlook. The astonishing cohesion of the Indian army was, and undoubtedly still is, mainly due to the superior status the soldier had among his fellow villagers.

The authorities in Delhi had recently come to realize that minor difficulties with the frontier tribes could be dealt with more effectively by bribery than by army action. The district Residents were given powers to pay the maliks, or headmen, to appoint their own "khassadars," or local policemen, whose pay would be stopped if any awkward incident occurred involving nontribal folk. It soon became clear, though, that the new policy was becoming so successful that the khassadars were having little to do. My general, Kenneth Wigram, a lively man with independent ideas (his brother was King George's private secretary), adopted a still more forward policy. He encouraged us, his British officers, to go out on rambles anywhere in the mountains, provided we were accompanied by two khassadars, each armed, by tribal custom, with a rifle and a knife. It would, of course, have been safer and more interesting if one of us could speak a little Pushtu. Fortunately, one of my officers was learning the language and was happy to practice it. We would scramble to a mountaintop, nine or ten thousand feet up, ascending crumbly rock slopes, barren except for a sparse covering by a kind of holly oak. Once, I was sitting on a rock during lunch and the subject of the Pathan knife came up. A khassadar began to explain, waving his knife in demonstration, just how he would disembowel an enemy. "You stab him low in the belly before thrusting upward—this avoids trouble with the ribs." He began to get overly excited, so we interrupted by expressing interest in the knife itself. Having got hold of it, we felt rather safer.

Early in 1930 an ambitious tribal leader named Zungi began to air grievances and make threats. The Resident could not deal with the problem, so he called in the army before the trouble could spread, as it had often done in the past. Zungi had had the enterprise to make a primitive field gun, and with it he started shelling the Jandola fort with solid lumps of mild steel. Having no understanding of artillery, their range finding was done by moving the gun forward or backward instead of tilting it up or down. The steel slugs fell about harmlessly.

Wigram sent out the usual punitive army column. Their objective was the destruction of one or two watchtowers in the offender's main village. I never discovered any modern purpose for these tall watchtowers. They undoubtedly were important as prestige symbols. Previously, our punitive columns had kept in touch by reeling out miles of field cable through the mountains. The tribesmen routinely cut the cable and then picked off the men who came along to mend it. I suggested to Wigram that this was old-fashioned nonsense, for the radio we now carried had improved a lot since the cat's whisker days of the First World War and was quite reliable.

Moreover, the absence of the customary cable would surprise and disappoint the enemy. So our column, operating in apparent isolation, demonstrated for the first time that the field cable was quite unnecessary. Zungi soon surrendered and accepted the retribution imposed on his people.

Our little war being over, I took a short holiday in Kashmir with one of Wigram's staff officers. We took my car. Getting to Kashmir involved either chancing that the precarious valley road along the Jhelum River would be free of landslides and open to traffic, or driving over the ten-thousand-foot Banihal Pass. We chose the pass, the way the old Mogul emperors once took their entire courts on trains of elephants to avoid the summer heat of Delhi. The road clung to cliff walls above a precipice. There was no curb on the outside, the brink being marked only by single upright rocks spaced two or three car lengths apart. It was foggy and the road was wet and muddy. We were quite alone, having passed no one for many miles. Rounding a bluff, I looked down and caught sight of the Jhelum as a silver ribbon far below. Then suddenly we were blinded by a belt of dense fog and began to skid helplessly outward. In another second we would have been over the edge, but a miracle happened as the outside front wheel hit something with a violent blow. The car slid around back into the road and came to a stop. By a one-in-a-thousand chance we had not only hit a boundary rock, but we hit it in just the right place to have it deflect us inward. Ever afterward I have been interested in probability.

The state of Kashmir was then still owned by a masterful maharaja determined to exclude unwanted tourists. The country therefore had remained largely unspoilt. Needou's little hotel in Srinagar was welcoming and comfortable. We saw the famous lake with its floating gardens. I bought a set of small tables that were finely carved from perfectly seasoned walnut obtained in the state forests. Today they still have no warp or cracks. In that clear alpine atmosphere, surrounded by mountains, the Vale of Kashmir seemed a fairyland. As in the Alps, one feels capable of anything. One after-noon I scrambled several thousand feet up a hillside to the winter ski slope of Gulmerg. There was snow on the ground. From that height I looked to the northwest and saw a solitary snow summit that looked quite close. It was Nanda Parbat, the fourth-highest mountain in the world, a hundred miles away.

I was lucky to have been sent to Waziristan, away from the heat of the Indian plains and the claustrophobic sense of being surrounded by 300 million people. We had a fair experience of that heat, though. My base was in an old fort on the west bank of the Indus, some six hundred miles inland from the river's mouth. All summer the tem-perature remained around 110°F at night, with extra humidity from the great river. During the long summer flood season the Indus was several miles wide and swirled around and between a crowd of small islands. There were no bridges here; the closest one was a hundred miles or so farther upriver. One crossed over into India on the SS *Blossom,* a venerable paddle steamer. The journey across took up to seven hours of almost unbearable humidity while the ship fought against the current.

The climate in the Waziristan mountains is peculiar. In contrast to the intense blue sky of the Himalayan foothills to the east, the Waziristan sky is usually obscured by a blanket of yellow haze out of which might come, unpredictably, sunshine or a deluge of rain or hailstones the size of large gooseberries. Owing to the hail, there are neither gardens nor crops. A military road crossed the flat, quarter-mile-wide dry bed of the Tochi River. I was once driving down the bank to cross this flat when a loud roar suddenly burst out, seemingly from close upstream. I looked up and saw a high wall of dark brown water emerging from a nearby side valley. Within seconds the whole riverbed was drowned under a raging torrent some six feet deep. Great boulders bounced along like cro-quet balls. Had I started a minute earlier, both car and I would have disappeared. Yet there had been no warning threat of rain or darkening sky—the water must have come from a cloudburst confined to that side valley.

I suppose it was that sort of thing, together with the fact of living in tribal territory beyond the Indian pale, that had led to the tradition that we must be given special privileges of three months' leave instead of two. We were also given a mileage traveling allowance so large that I was able to live on it without spending any of my pay. Wigram once expostulated mildly about that allowance but was politely told to shut up.

On the whole, I had very little health trouble. I did get a bad go of malaria at Jubbulpore with a temperature of 105°F. They treated me with a pair of brand-new drugs, Atabrine and Plasmoquin, which had to be taken separately. (The medical orderly once came to my bed excitedly waving a test tube: "Look what I've found. I've mixed the two and they've set like cement.") I was given some weeks to convalesce, so I motored to Simla to do some good walking, eight thousand feet up in the foothills of the Himalayas. On returning, I happened to meet my army doctor who asked where I had been. When I told him, his jaw dropped: "Good God, you ought to be dead. I must have forgotten to warn you that you should be very careful and undertake as little exercise as possible for some weeks after taking those drugs."

Another time I had noticed a tiny spot on the back of my left hand. After a few months it changed to a hole in the skin that grew bigger and bigger until it was two inches across. It was quite painless, and I could lift up the surrounding skin and look underneath. All the doctors could say was, "There is no known cure. You are lucky it hasn't started on your face." I heard of a keen young radiologist up in Rawalpindi with a special X-ray machine just out from England. The doctors were skeptical and talked of X-ray burns. But I went to see the radiologist anyway, and he thought the thing could be killed if he used just the right dose, starting gingerly. He covered my arm and the rest of my hand with massive lead screens and switched on the X-ray. There was an explosion and much smoke.

"Damned termites," he said, "they keep on eating the insulation." We got down with screwdrivers and insulation tape, found the short circuit, and replaced the blown fuse. The first low dose had no effect, but the second, ten days later and slightly stronger, completely killed the thing without doing me any damage. New scar tissue began to grow inward from the edges. I am very grateful to that young man.

An Alsatian's life is mainly watching, remembering, and anticipating. A week or so before I would go away on a long leave, Cubby would begin to suspect it from watching Shafiullah's actions. When quite sure, he would desert me. I was told by friends that he went house hunting. He was a great favorite and many would have been happy to look after him, but it was he who did the choosing. While I was away he must have continued to watch Shafiullah, for he was always there to greet me when I returned. Sadly, Cubby died of rabies, probably caught from a jackal or hyena.

I returned to England early in 1931 at the end of my overseas tour. I liked India and its people and was sorry to leave. In spite of the summer heat, I can still recall with nostalgia the bird and cicada sounds and the jungle smells.

7

Family and an Expedition to the Sudan

MY MOTHER DIED suddenly in 1931 from a massive cerebral hemorrhage. She had had high blood pressure for many years but tried to conceal it. She had always been a darling to Enid and me, though I had been away off and on for a number of years. Her death came as a great shock, for it happened during a small birthday party for her grandson Tucker Jones. From laughter and enjoyment, she just had time to cry out "Arth . . ." before she was gone. For her, it was the ideal way to die. My father, aged seventy-six, took the loss stoically, but he was very lonely. They had always been very close. Enid managed to find an almost perfect companion-housekeeper, Mrs. Scott-Higgins, who remained with him at Warren Wood until he died in 1944 in his ninetieth year.

In the middle of the nineteenth century, my grandfather William Henry Alger and his close friend Robert Burnard (accent on the last syllable) started a chemical fertilizer business in Plymouth. They also had a deep-water wharf fronting Cattewater Inlet, a warehouse, and a branch railway into the facility. Behind the warehouse lay a honeycomb of old vertical-sided limestone quarries whence had come most of the stone of Old Plymouth. As a boy, I had often been taken round the works by my uncle Harold, W. H. Alger's son. The firm imported iron pyrite, which was roasted to give off sulphur dioxide. This was sprayed with water in great lead-lined chambers to form sulphuric acid. Phosphates were also imported and used to make "superphosphate" for the Devon farmers.

The business prospered until after the First World War, when it ran into serious competition from bigger firms like ICI, Fisions, and so on. By that time both co-founders had died and had been succeeded by their sons, Lawrence Burnard and Harold Alger. The new owners decided on a complete reconstruction. The chemical works were scrapped, and the firm restricted its business to acting as wharfinger. The old timber pilings and top decking of the wharf were replaced, stage by stage, by a ferroconcrete structure. As neither Lawrence nor Harold had any construction experience, my father, an in-law member of the Alger family, was called in and made a director. Messrs. Rendel, Palmer, and Triton, then the leaders in ferroconcrete wharf construction, were appointed consulting engineers for the job. The new wharf allowed ships of deep draught to use it, and this attracted two oil companies to establish depots and tank farms in the old quarries. This brought in permanent business over and above that of our general cargo customers.

With the reconstruction, the firm's name was changed from Burnard and Alger to Cattedown Wharves, Ltd. I suppose that in terms of turnover, the wharfinger business is one of the least labour intensive. We employed only sixteen stevedores, reliable local men who had worked for us for many years. The office staff consisted of the secretary, a lifelong company servant to whom we owed a great deal, and his young understudy. Our only outside commitment was our responsibility, as Cattewater Commissioners, to employ a local dredging contractor to keep the channel clear. It remained a nice little business, limited in scope but secure and lucrative.

By the articles of association, the shares were held equally between the Burnard and Alger families. There were four directors, one of whom acted by mutual consent as manager. After the reconstruction, the directors were Lawrence Burnard, his son Jack, Uncle

Harold, and my father. On my return from India I became an alternate to my father and attended the directors' meetings. Later, when Father retired, I became director in his place. After each meeting in the little wharf office, we would adjourn to the Royal Western Yacht Club for a splendid lunch, followed by a stoop of port (a very large glass). We owed this ritual to Uncle Harold, who in his younger days had been a keen yachtsman.

I used to love those visits to the west country, scene of many fond childhood memories. I always stayed with Uncle Harold and Aunt Mabel at Filham House, a small jewel of a place near Ivybridge on the southern edge of Dartmoor. It was a miniature medieval mansion containing a small great hall with a minstrel gallery. It was kept spotless by two ancient retainers and smelt of peat and heather. Outside was a lake owned by two friendly swans. Once I found one of them asleep in the drawing room, in the best armchair. Beyond the lake lay a park of about forty acres, let to a local farmer for grazing. Just outside the house a small stream gurgled down a bank from the moors to feed the lake. The open moor was just one field gate away, and I would put on stout boots and scramble up through granite rocks and heather to the top of Ughborough Beacon, whence I could see most of South Devon. Aunt Mabel's hospitality was of the lavish South Devon kind. There were bowls of clotted cream from a nearby farm, and the breakfast sideboard was loaded with porridge, fish, eggs or kidneys, and bacon.

In due course Lawrence Burnard retired; he died before the Second World War. During the destruction of Plymouth in the war, Uncle Harold, then well over seventy, was to be found running the business from the mouth of a draughty railway tunnel. Sometime in the 1960s Uncle Harold also retired, so Cattedown Wharves, Ltd., fell into the hands of the third generation, Jack Burnard and myself. Jack was an excellent managing director, and the company continued to prosper for a number of years until he in turn wanted to retire. There were then no other members of either family willing and capable of taking over. Rather than face the uncertainty of bringing in some outsider, we decided to sell (of course with the agreement of all family members). Jack found a shipowner from among his business acquaintances who was anxious to buy and willing to pay what was at the time a very good price.

On my return to England from India in 1931 I became chief instructor at the School of Signals at Catterick. I found life in England tame and narrow after Egypt and India. Just then, especially, I needed some potent distraction. By pure chance I happened to see Bill Shaw in the map room of the Royal Geographical Society. In front of him was an open map of northeast Africa. We both had the same thought. Memories of the old thrills of exploration were still very strong—driving into unknown and unmapped country where perhaps no one had been since Stone Age people left due to lack of water; the thrill of finding oneself alone among their implements and the ashes of their ancient hearths.

The whole of the northern Sudan west of the Nile was uninhabited; it was mapped only vaguely in bedouin terms of camel-day distances and "Polaris-over-left-shoulder" bearings. There were stories of unlocated oases and water holes. An ambitious plan began to germinate: we would traverse the unexplored frontier region bordering the French province of Chad as far south as the edge of civilization. This would involve a cross-country journey of some six thousand miles. With the new Model-A Ford cars, an improved version of the Model-T, we could be entirely self-contained for fifteen hundred miles, so two separate dumps of petrol would have to be established at accessible places. This would require the cooperation of the governors of at least two provinces, as well as the Shell Oil Company people. There was as yet no airmail service to Egypt or the Sudan, so the arrangements took a long time.

The British government of the Sudan was only thirty years old, having started from scratch at the beginning of the century after the resettlement. Rightly reserving its slender revenues for the populated rain-fed south, the government had largely neglected the empty desert of the north. Therefore it was ill-equipped to deal with a recent succession of raids on the northern Nile-bank villages and on caravans by a band of outlaws coming from somewhere far away in the mysterious west, out of reach of the Sudan Defence Force. In consequence, the government was happy to help us in any way they could, at any rate in the regions under its control. The existence of this band of raiders meant that we would have to be adequately armed. Owing to this and the length of the journey, I reckoned that we should be a party of eight in four cars.

We started from Cairo as planned in the autumn of 1932. The party consisted of Bill Shaw; myself; Dr. Kenneth Sandford, an Oxford geologist; Major Hugh Boustead, who commanded the Western Camel Corps and thus represented the government; Guy Prendergast; and Lieutenant R. N. Harding-Newman of the Royal Tank Corps and two other young officers who were serving in Egypt at that time. This time the GOC made no difficulties. Being on the spot, Prendergast was able to buy four car chassis and have our special bodies fitted to them, and he was there to deal with the myriad other details involved in such an expedition.

Ever since my Cambridge days I had used a simple accounting system in which each person recorded everything he personally spent toward the joint cost. Afterward, all such expenditures were added together and divided by the number of participants. It was then easy to adjust the individual differences to equalize everyone's share. After both this and the 1930 expedition, I was able to recoup and distribute nearly all our expenditures from payments I received for descriptive articles written for *The Times*. An account of our expeditions up to and including that of 1932 is given in *Libyan Sands: Travel in a Dead World*, written in 1933–34 while I was in Hong Kong. I remember nothing of writing it, for the chapters seemed to follow one another without need of significant revisions. It was published in 1935 by Hodder and Stoughton, who also printed a pocket edition in 1941. It was republished in 1987 by Michael Haag, Ltd., of London, so after many years it is back in print.

I will mention here only a few incidents from that 1932 expedition, including one that had a bearing on future events and another that illustrates the simple, commonsense expediency of the Sudan

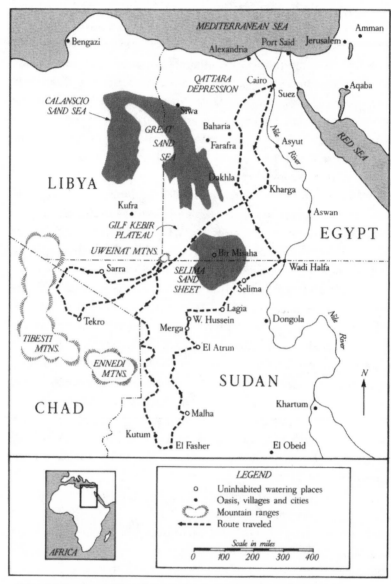

2. Map of the eastern Sahara showing the route of the 1932 expedition.
The 3,700 miles covered made it the longest expedition in the eastern Sahara at that time.

Civil Service. Our first objective was the isolated mountain mass of Uweinat, eight hundred miles southwest of Cairo and at the exact meeting point of the Egyptian-Libyan and Egyptian-Sudan frontiers. The six-thousand-foot mountain attracts its own local rainfall, and good water could be got from an underground pool. According to British maps this pool was definitely situated within Sudanese territory. We approached cautiously, for there was a chance that the band of raiders might be camping there. Instead, we found the Italian army established with tents, aircraft, and transport vehicles. The colonel in charge greeted us in an offhand, noncommittal way. He clearly had doubts about the legality of his presence and was surprised at being discovered, but we parted amicably. At Sarra Well, two hundred miles farther west, we came on another Italian detachment commanded by a very different type, a real desert enthusiast like ourselves who had served in Libya for some years. Major Lorenzini invited us to dinner that night and produced a sumptuous meal served on upturned petrol drums and lit by the headlights of his transport. We had a lively talk about the capabilities of motor transport in this desert, in the course of which he said, "The Nile at Aswan is only nine hundred kilometers from Uweinat. If there is a war, what fun it would be to take a battalion to Aswan and seize the dam. What could you do?" I am quite sure neither of us at that time had the slightest inkling that any real war was likely to involve Libya, but both Lorenzini and his remark impressed me. I knew how easily such a long-distance raid could be done, and Lorenzini seemed just the man to do it.

Although the whole of Libya had been ceded to Italy as early as 1904, they had barely been able to hold onto the Mediterranean coast. Senussi tribesmen dominated the interior. Finally, the Italian government decided on a stronger line and in 1931 mounted a well-organized expedition which succeeded in occupying Kufra Oasis, the Senussi stronghold, without a fight. The officers we met had taken part and, flushed with success, had pushed on farther south until, in the British view, they had overstepped the Sudan frontier. I reported this intrusion to the Foreign Office in London as soon as possible. There followed two years of diplomatic wrangling, during which it emerged that no frontier between Libya and the Sudan had ever been internationally agreed upon. When the Foreign Office learned that the disputed region contained nothing but lifeless sand, it was decided that if Italy really wanted sand, she could have it. The frontier on British maps was changed accordingly.

From the desert of absolute lifelessness, we passed through areas of gradually increasing wildlife, first solitary addax, the rarest of all antelopes and the origin of the unicorn myth, then herds of oryx, followed by ostrich flocks, baboons, and finally man. We came at last to Kutum, the northernmost administrative centre. Here a lonely young district officer made us very welcome. We had a lot of repacking and refurbishing to do, so he thoughtfully provided a chain gang of prisoners to help. They were in the charge of another prisoner, unchained. I expressed some doubt about this, but our young host assured us, "That will be perfectly safe. The chap in charge is completely reliable. He's a murderer." The logic was not readily apparent, but we learned later that the man had merely killed his wife's seducer. The law said he must go to prison, but if he had *not* killed the man, in the eyes of his tribe he would have committed an unpardonable moral crime. As a fair compromise, this decent, upright man was made foreman, and as such retained his tribal status. Everyone was content with this arrangement.

Another small incident concerned the sense of smell. We had been driving for several hundred miles on a compass bearing across the great Selima Sand Sheet, toward a little uninhabited oasis where we expected to find a dump of petrol placed there by a caravan organized by Shell. It was to be guarded by a policeman. It was getting dark, and we were very tired. As we should have been nearing the oasis, I omitted the usual position finding by astrofix. In the early morning I distinctly smelt camel. There was a gentle breeze blowing from the northeast. As it was most unlikely there could be any other camels within a hundred miles or more, I decided to drive blindly on the smell. We drove on for eight miles, and there, in a small depression out of sight from any distance, was the little oasis, the petrol, the policeman, and his camel. One knows that even the human sense of smell can at times be very sensitive, but it is surprising that the presence of that one animal could be detected eight miles away.

The return journey followed several hundred miles of the ancient Darb el Arba'in, the desert slave route. It used to take the great slave caravans forty days to traverse this route. The way was marked by tens of thousands of camel skeletons scattered along a belt some ten miles wide. There were no car tracks, so we must have been the first to travel along the route in many years. The slave traffic ceased with the Sudan rebellion of 1884. Sadly, no information exists as to how those huge caravans, involving several thousand black slaves, were organized, and how that host of humans and camels was fed and watered.

Some time later a report filtered through to Khartoum that Gongoi, the leader of the desert raiders, had been killed in a quarrel with his brother, and the gang of raiders had dispersed shortly before our expedition got to those regions. So the nightly armed watch we kept had been unnecessary. It appears that the gang had been desperate outlaws from across the Chad frontier—very primitive Guraan people who worshipped certain tree stumps. They had terrified the Nile-bank villagers, who had cried for help, saying they had been attacked by beings who lived on snakes and whose camels needed no water and made no hoof prints in the sand. It is possible that the raiders had reached Lagia Oasis and, finding no wildlife there for food, had left their camels and walked to the Nile. We found nothing at Lagia except, unaccountably, a man's severed leg. Incidentally, our astrofix position moved Lagia from one map sheet to another.

The Royal Geographical Society had given us much encouragement in our efforts to explore the remoter parts of the Libyan Desert. They provided small financial grants and loaned us surveying instruments. In 1934 the Society was good enough to award me their Gold Medal for what we had accomplished.

8

The Far East
1933–1934

I WAS NEVER a "keen soldier" in the sense of having high rank as my primary objective, and I had no wish to compete for the Staff College. As a boy I had taken an army career as an engineer for granted, as a family tradition. Later, I used to say openly that I would rather become an FRS (Fellow of the Royal Society) than a major general. The keen soldiers tended to wangle a succession of home postings so as to be noticed. Overseas postings were therefore easily obtainable. I preferred to see the world rather than soldier in England.

In 1933 there happened to be a vacancy as OC Signals China Command. I applied for and got it. I duly arrived in Hong Kong by sea and decided to live in the Peninsula Hotel in Kowloon on the mainland side of the great harbor. The job consisted of looking after scattered signal detachments in Singapore, Hong Kong, Shanghai, Tientsin, and at the embassy in Peking. It involved a lot of traveling by sea, up and down the China coast. Each detachment formed a part of the token British military presence securing the main international trading ports from possible Chinese interference. The Chinese central government, traditionally archaic and more recently revolutionary, was kept unstable by the presence of several roving warlords. The main security of the international China trade rested by agreement on the British navy. A cruiser was stationed off Shanghai, and another in the far interior, fifteen hundred miles up the Yangtze River.

Now that Britain has given up a worldwide empire, one realizes on looking back that for years we had held on to the outlying parts of it by mere tradition and the apparent absence of any imminent threat. The farther away from England, the more out-of-date and ineffective were the land defenses. Repeated demands for replacements of antiquated equipment received the same standard answer, "Agreed in principle, but no funds available." One could only keep one's unit well trained and content.

Captain Henderson, my second in command, and I clubbed together and bought a yacht, a three-and-a-half-ton cabin cruiser, and engaged a Chinese boat boy to look after it. Hong Kong is an ideal place to sail, and there are many beautiful spots on the nearby coast where one could stop to picnic. It was quite safe provided one was careful to watch for typhoon warnings and avoided straying beyond British-controlled waters into areas liable to piracy. We took part in the usual yacht-club events. Neither Henderson nor I had done any sailing before, but on one occasion at least we won a trophy, much to the annoyance of the older and more serious members who affected yachting caps and correct uniforms.

I happened one day to run into a Chinese fellow student from Cambridge days. He invited me and two or three other Cambridge men to dinner in Canton. I discovered to my astonishment that he was the mayor of that city. He met us at the frontier with a big official car and was dressed in the high-buttoned uniform of a commissar. At a traffic holdup in the suburbs of Canton, a beggar appeared at the open window on his side of the car. Our host snapped the window shut. I heard him mutter, half apologetically, "Wretches. I got rid of two hundred of them only last week." "Got rid of" meant they had been liquidated. However, he was an excellent host. We had an amusing and very interesting evening, and a delightful meal, on the fifth floor of a bamboo hotel, reached by a curious lift that swayed from side to side. Coming away, rather late, the city seemed as busy as during the day. "We're not like you," he said, "business in my city goes on night and day."

During the last century the name Hong Kong was confined to the island, a ridge of crumbling rock seven miles long and rising to fourteen hundred feet. Following the China Wars, waged mainly by Britain to gain freedom of trade, the island was given to Britain in perpetuity by the emperor. This was done as a gesture of contempt, it being thought utterly useless to anyone. However, lying a mile off the mainland, Hong Kong shelters one of the finest harbours in the world. Moreover, the rock was easily cut away and pushed into the sea to create new land for buildings. The town of Victoria appeared, into which a Chinese population peacefully swarmed, and young Jardine established his first warehouse, or "go-down." At the end of the century the New Territories on the opposite mainland were obtained on a ninety-nine year lease. This provided more land for development, together with an adequate water supply, which was previously lacking.

The importance of the now-expanded trading colony lay in its nearness by both land and water to the great Chinese city of Canton and its surrounding markets. But as with the other treaty ports along the coast, trading with foreigners was confined to local sale and exchange, traffic with the interior being left entirely in Chinese hands. Thus the great trading firms like Jardine Matheson associated themselves with a Chinese partner, or compradore, some of whom became millionaires. The system allowed trade to be carried on, although Chinese territory was virtually out-of-bounds to foreigners.

In those days the international settlement in Shanghai was still flourishing. The community of foreign traders, their families, and their great business offices were confined by the Celestial Empire to a small enclave within the vast Chinese city. The settlement had been sited on a marsh, allocated disdainfully by a former emperor. Buildings, however tall, were founded on concrete rafts, so designed that the ground floors were initially several feet too high. The final weight of the completed structure caused just the right amount of sinkage to place the building at ground level.

The community of British, French, German, American, and Japanese was self-governing by treaty and beyond the jurisdiction of the Chinese government. It had its own formidable police force, manned by tall, bearded and turbaned Sikhs. Under the compradore system, the great trading firms like Jardine Matheson and Sassoons lived and grew rich entirely within the bounds of the settlement, in the security of one British cruiser of the Far Eastern Fleet. Few of the inhabitants ever strayed across the boundary street into the outer city. China was an unreal, painted background to their lives.

The settlement was enormously wealthy. Land values along the main street were higher than in the city of London. The Shanghai Club boasted of the longest bar in the world. There were plenty of sporting facilities. European political quarrels seemed remote and inexplicable when viewed from the garden of the tennis club, in the company of friends of various nationalities. International peace and understanding comes naturally in an isolated community permanently under a potential threat from just across the street. At that time, large Chinese armies were marching about the interior, and as a precaution the settlement had recently been strengthened by a brigade of British troops.

I had hung a large-scale map of Asia on the wall of my room, and I dreamed of driving a car from China to Turkestan and Europe. It might be just possible, except for politics. I wanted to find out. On a visit to Peking I met Owen Lattimore, the American explorer. He told me that the whole of the caravan trade, mainly in furs, was in the hands of the Scandinavians. They knew the northern country better than anyone. Indeed, I had already talked to Nils Horner, a former member of Sven Hedin's central Asia expedition. By luck I also met a young Swede named Oberg, who invited me to spend a weekend at his home at Kweiwa, way up on the Mongolian border. A long train journey was involved. Our embassy kindly provided me with a beautifully illuminated passport in Chinese characters.

I boarded a wagon-lit in Peking on a hot May evening. I was the only foreign passenger. There was a lot of stopping and reversing during the night. Opening my window early next morning, the air felt surprisingly cold. We were going along a river valley. The river was frozen, and there was no vegetation to be seen. To our one sleeping coach there was now attached a long coal train. We had climbed six thousand feet during the night and had called at the Kalgan coal mines on the edge of the Mongolian plateau. Sometime during the morning the train was stopped and boarded by the army of some local warlord. A young officer, smartly dressed, entered my compartment. After inspecting me curiously, he clearly demanded something. I offered him my illuminated passport. He waved that aside. What else could he want? I gave him one of the visiting cards I had had printed in Chinese. He smiled gratefully and saluted. He just wanted a souvenir. He had probably never seen a foreigner before.

The train arrived at Kweiwa late that afternoon. Oberg met me and drove to his home. He was the son of a missionary, had lived at Kweiwa most of his life, spoke the local languages fluently, and was employed as an intermediary between the caravans, the bandits, and the government. An elderly English couple, well educated and interesting to talk to, were also staying at his home. They were Buddhists and were negotiating with Oberg to escort them to Tibet, where they wished to die. Oberg told me he was against the venture. The journey would be dangerous because of bandits, and the attitude of the Panchen Lama was uncertain. On the other hand, I gathered that the fee offered was enormous.

I asked him what the winters were like here. He said the temperature often fell to −40°C, with a howling wind. I asked how he coped with that. His answer: "I go to bed and stay there." His bed was a brick affair with a stove underneath.

One of the highlights of my Far East tour occurred during the few weeks' leave I took to visit Indochina via Singapore. The journey started rather oddly. My sea booking to Singapore happened to involve changing to another liner at Manila. I embarked from Hong Kong in the *Empress of Canada,* one of the great liners of the time. The ship seemed strangely empty. I drifted to the huge first-class saloon for dinner and found myself to be the only passenger. However, the complete staff was there to wait on me, and the full Philippino band was playing. This routine continued for the whole three-day voyage to Manila. I have rarely felt so self-conscious. Apparently the *Empress* was to take on a full load of American tourists returning to the United States from the Philippines.

I traveled northward from Singapore by train, through the twelve hundred miles of Malaya to Bangkok. I had a sleeping compartment provided with a private sitting room and bathroom, and a bed complete with mosquito netting. The train, drawn by the latest diesel-electric locomotive, hurried through rubber plantations and pineapple and rice fields. Except for the unusual luxury of my quarters, I had begun to conclude that one Far Eastern country was very like the next. But at the Siamese capital, opening the centre pages of the *Bangkok Times,* I read:

Court Circular
Grand Palace, 7 November 2476

Yesterday afternoon, His Royal highness the Prince Patriarch proceeded to the Hall of Amarinda, and, on behalf of His Majesty the King, presented Royal Warrants conferring various ranks upon seventy-seven priests.

Thereafter His Highness Prince Devawongse represented His Majesty The King at the consecration of the image of Our Lord Buddha which had recently been cast for the coming anniversary of His Majesty's birthday. This morning His Highness Prince Devawongse was again present at the Hall of Amarinda where food was presented to the priests who took part in yesterday's services. A sermon was preached by the Most Reverend Somdech Phra Buddhakopsacharia of Debairindra Monastery. Thereafter His Highness presented customary gifts to the priests.

Today being the anniversary of His Majesty The King, the army and navy each fired a Royal Salute of twenty-one guns. In the afternoon His

Highness Prince Devawongse lit candles and incense in worship of the
Emerald Buddha. A chapter of five priests then celebrated a special service consisting of nine special sets of texts from Holy Scripture, and
Royal Astrologers alternately recited propitiatory incantations to the
nine tutelaries. While this was in progress His Highness proceeded to
the Royal Pantheon to pay homage to His Majesty's august predeces-
sors. Thereafter His Highness proceeded to the Hall of Amarinda where
a chapter of sixty priests performed a religious service in celebration of
His Majesty's birthday.

It read like a translation from some ancient manuscript. The railway station with its diesel-electric locomotives seemed to fade
away.

Being the only independent sovereign of a purely Buddhist state,
His Majesty the King of Siam was, and I suppose still is, the protec-
tor of the Buddhist faith. He alone was allowed to disrobe the Emerald Buddha in the royal palace and change its clothes three times
a year according to the seasons. The Siamese temples are astonishing from the outside. Their variously shaped elaborate spires, all
sheathed with pieces of coloured glass, seem to blaze and scintillate
in a heavenly way. Bangkok is all fairly new. The old capital farther
up the Menom River was destroyed two centuries ago by the Burmese. A few centuries before that the Siamese themselves had destroyed what remained of the great empire of the Khmers, whose
capital seems to have been Angkor in Cambodia. The White Elephant, which I saw in the palace stables, is given annually to the
Burmese as traditional tribute. It is an albino; however, as elephants
have very little hair, it was rather disappointing. There were a great
many priests about in their yellow robes and with their traditional
begging bowls. Most of them would be better described as undergraduates, for every young man aspires to wear the yellow robe for
a year or so in order to join the fraternity. Siamese Buddhism is the
newer reformed religion imported centuries ago from Ceylon. It is the
Hinayana, or "little way," as opposed to the Mahayana, or "great
way," which became largely absorbed by the Hindu divinities.

Siam seemed a happy country. The people are pleasant, lazy, and law-abiding. Like the Japanese, they take to Western customs easily, but unlike the Japanese they seem incapable of organizing anything. The peasants work the fields. The Siamese nobility rule them. The Europeans do the organizing, and the Chinese do the trading. It all seems to work well in normal times.

I was charmed by Bangkok, the Venice of the East. The canals (klongs) are kept clean by the flowing river water and thronged with canoes, sampans, and little houseboats, all very busy. Fruit shops abounded, selling every kind of luscious tropical fruit. Above a shop one sometimes found a little theatre showing an old-time play with princes and princesses in traditional royal costumes. I saw a number of lepers about—no one seemed anxious to avoid them.

A drive of a hundred miles in a French car owned by a Cambodian gentleman and driven by an Annamite took me across the frontier to Angkor in French Indochina. Here there were no railways. The French had omitted that stage of transportation, going straight from hand porterage to motor roads. The French manager of a little bungalow hotel close to the ruins made me most comfortable, considering the sweltering heat. The food was excellent, and I ate outdoors under the trees. The country was steamy hot and consisted of swamps and forests full of swarms of flying insects. The mosquitoes bit ferociously. At dinner, flies swarmed round the lantern hung from a tree and were dashed to the ground by the blades of a fan rotating above. Underneath sat a wide circle of large, warty toads, eating the flies as they fell. As I sat down to dine, the toads looked up, smiled, and went on eating.

The Khmer ruins cover a great forested area. The old people thought nothing of building artificial lakes ten miles long, contained within raised bunds. The French had driven roads through the forest to most of the old sites. The great Angkor Wat temple had been cleared of jungle and was well maintained, but many others were still strangled by forest trees and vines, much as they had been when they were found in 1860. The so-called buttress tree, which

seems to be attracted by the ruins, is a giant, soft-wooded growth
that supports itself by three huge roots that jut out like buttresses.
These huge green-white roots are like octopus tentacles that spread
over and under stone roofs and squeeze miraculously through the
joints of walls without displacing any of the stonework. Roots a
foot or more in diameter glide along dark corridors and then disappear suddenly into stone floors. These soft, yielding tentacles have
crept over whole temples. In one spot a head of Buddha, twenty feet
across, stuck out of the ground like the Great Sphinx. All that was
visible of its face was a bit around the eyes peering out of a hole
between the pale roots of a tree growing on top of the head. I saw a
high wall, still intact, running straight through the trunk of a great
tree that had grown up covering both sides. It is amazing how such
huge trees can be so gentle as they grow, swelling yet yielding to
the slightest touch against a poised coping stone. It is entirely owing to these peculiar trees that the great edifice of Angkor Wat remained intact through the centuries instead of crumbling to nothing
under the rank vegetation.

The huge temple rises tier upon tier of roofed cloisters, crowned
by three cloistered towers around a single holy-of-holies. Inside
each tier is a complicated maze of corridors and halls. The joints
between the sandstone blocks of the building were, I noticed,
stepped and halved as though the method had been copied without
change from that of a previous wooden period. The slavish copying
of woodwork in stone—a very unsound idea—by the Khmer archi-
tects of a few hundred years ago reminded me of what the ancient
Egyptians had done five thousand years ago in Zozer's time. The
roofs of those long cloisters were supported by hundreds of six-foot
sandstone columns which had evidently been turned on some sort
of lathe.

The cloister walls were covered with delicately carved bas-reliefs,
mostly of naked human figures about twenty centimeters high, together with intricate floral designs. As each of the four sides of the
bottom tier is half a kilometre long, there must be acres of these

bas-reliefs. The main theme seemed to be undisguised and inno-
cently normal sex. Parents were pictured going for a stroll, leading
their children by their genitals. Far above, the single chamber of the
holy-of-holies contained nothing but one huge phallus. Amazing
effort and patience must have been put into the laborious and detailed carving of these thousands upon thousands of finely finished
bas-reliefs. But why?

A moat fifty yards wide had been excavated to surround this
enormous edifice. The massive balustrade which edges the causeway across the moat is a continuous stone-carved serpent, a foot in
diameter, supported by rows of sturdy slaves. The water in the moat
was covered with pink water lilies in full flower. In a far corner,
French police elephants were bathing. The whole temple and its
surroundings gave the impression of having resulted from a single
concept that arose in the brain of some master architect and then
was executed without modification or addition. If it had existed in
classical times, it would certainly have been classed as one of the
Wonders of the World.

No one is likely to see Angkor again as I saw it, when it was still
thoughtfully maintained by the French curators. It has doubtless
been hopelessly defaced and wrecked during the ruthless wars in
Cambodia. It may well have been an artillery target.

I traveled by bus from Angkor to the Cambodian capital of
Phnom Penh, located at the junction of the Angkor waterway with
the great Mekong River. I crossed the Mekong on a rickety wooden
ferry and thence, next day, continued on to the French city of Sai-
gon. I returned to Hong Kong in a Chinese ship. The only Europeans on board were the seedy, rather down-at-heel British captain
and myself. There was nominally a first-class region, but Chinese
peasantry swarmed everywhere, peering at me as though I was
some strange animal. That was the most squalid sea journey I have
ever made.

I felt increasingly unwell during the last six months of my stay in
the Far East. Something inside had gone wrong. The doctors finally

decided I had "tropical sprue," the only known treatment for which was an immediate return to England and a period of almost complete starvation. I was allowed a little yoghurt, plus, for weeks on end, nothing but a tomato or so a day. I was later promoted to a banana. The troopship's iron cow produced the best yoghurt I have ever eaten. I arrived home in May 1934 and spent some further time in the military hospital at Millbank. I was later discharged as a permanent invalid, entirely lacking in digestive stomach acid. I was told that for the rest of my life I should have to take hydrochloric acid tablets with every meal.

9

Physics of Blown Sand
1935–1939

AS A BOY I had been excited by H. G. Wells's romances in science fiction, then only recently published. They stimulated me with the idea that there were new, unimagined things still to be discovered. Charles Philips had guided my early interest in science. The geographical explorations that I organized in Egypt and the Sudan were a first consequence. There might be something previously unknown just over the next horizon, not only in the geographical sense but much more generally. There were plenty of problems in physics, for instance, that remained unsolved. It was a theme I had thought about and tried to develop when I was writing the last chapter of *Libyan Sands* in Hong Kong.

In 1929 and 1930, during my weeks of travel over the lifeless sand sea in North Africa, I became fascinated by the vast scale of organization of the dunes and how a strong wind would cause the whole dune surface to flow, scouring sand from under one's feet. Here, where there existed no animals, vegetation, or rain to interfere with sand movements, the dunes seemed to behave like living things. How was it that they kept their precise shape while marching interminably downwind? How was it that they insisted on repairing any damage done to their individual shapes? How, in other regions of the same desert, were they able to breed "babies" just like themselves that proceeded to run on ahead of their parents? Why did they absorb nourishment and continue to grow instead of allowing the sand to spread out evenly over the desert as finer dust grains do? More basically, what kind of upward physical force must be exerted on the mineral grains to make them rise against the force of gravity, lifting them to such a height that they can strike one's face like little hammers? No satisfactory answers to these questions existed. Indeed, no one had investigated the physics of blown sand. So here was a new field, I thought, one that could be explored at home in England in laboratory-controlled conditions.

The army doctors' gloomy predictions were wrong. I recovered completely in a few months, with this absorbing new occupation in mind. I did some preliminary experiments on the physical properties of quartz sand grains in my father's little workshop on Shooters Hill. However, it was clear that I must build a special wind tunnel for what I wanted to do, and find room to house it. Professor C. M. White of Imperial College at South Kensington kindly let me have adequate space in his large hydraulics laboratory. I built the wind tunnel myself, of thin plywood, and installed an electric blower powerful enough to drive winds up to forty miles an hour through the tunnel. I also designed and made a number of special bits and pieces of equipment, including a wind-velocity probe made from a fine hypodermic syringe which could be used for measurements very close to the sand bed and within the dense cloud of moving grains. White gave me a great deal of helpful advice on the purely fluid-dynamic aspects of the processes. It was a time when the general velocity pattern of turbulent fluid flow past a rigid boundary was becoming known through the pioneering work of Ludwig Prandtl in Berlin, Theodor von Kármán, and others. But my problem concerned a wind boundary containing dispersed moving sand grains. Since by Newton's third law every action demands an equal and opposite reaction, it was clear that in moving the sand grains, the wind itself must be modified. I was dealing, in fact, with a new kind of flowing substance, one in which relatively massive solids are mixed with a fluid and in which the concentration of solids and the consequent resistance to motion increases with the applied shear stress. My wind-tunnel experiments showed that Prandtl's wind-velocity pattern still held, but in a definitely modified way. There followed an interesting correspondence with Professor Prandtl.

Other experiments showed that, as I had expected, quartz grains are so perfectly elastic and resistant to abrasion that in a strong wind they bounce upward like a football. I photographed this jumping, or "saltating," action of fast-moving grains in the intense light of an exploding electric arc which I rigged up. The bouncing motion implied that the height of rise must depend on the kind of impact the grains had with the ground. Evidently, for a certain rate of descent, a grain will bounce higher off a massive, rigid solid than off a yielding surface. The higher it rises, the faster the wind speed around it, so the faster it will be blown along. It followed that if the grains bounce off larger and less yielding bed grains rather than off grains of their own size, their mass transport rate will be greater. Experiments in the wind tunnel showed that blown grains of uniform size impact so violently with bed grains of the same size that little craters are made from which other bed grains are thrown up into the airstream, but only to a moderate height. This at once explained why dune sand tends to collect on surfaces of like size—the transport there is less than elsewhere.

As all natural sands are composed of a mixture of grains of different sizes, the need arose to examine the statistical distribution of the different sizes. By laborious sieving I analyzed many hundreds of samples from a wide range of natural deposits, including sands moved by winds, in rivers, and on the seabed. Sand was collected while in transit, as well as after accumulating in a deposit. On a plot of proportional frequency of occurrence of grains of any given size against a scale of size, the general distribution curve assumed the shape of a mound whose sides tailed off, gradually approaching zero at increasing distances on either side. The difficulty was that the measured frequencies along the tails became so small that they were unplottable. Not being a statistician, I concluded that this difficulty could be overcome simply by plotting the frequencies indirectly as their logarithms, thus giving every frequency, however small, an equal prominence. The precise pattern of the complete size distribution of a natural sand at once appeared. It consisted of two converging straight lines joined by a curved summit. The curve resembled a simple hyperbola.

This meant that on an ordinary linear plot, the tail frequencies on either side decayed exponentially, as do many other natural quantities. However, according to century-old tradition, the theoretical random distribution had been applied to quantities such as sand-grain sizes. On the semilog plot, that random distribution would resemble a parabola without straight-line tails, contrary to what I had found. Thus my sand size distributions, measured accurately for the first time, suggested that the traditional theory of randomness might be wrong. These statistical results attracted little or no interest at the time, but forty years later, when the method of logarithmic plotting was applied to distributions in other widely differing fields, the log-hyperbolic pattern appeared to be a general rather than an isolated phenomenon, and so to be of considerable philosophical interest.

Another important result of my wind-tunnel measurements was the finding that for a certain sand-grain size, the transport rate of blown sand varies as the cube of the wind-velocity gradient, just as the mechanical power produced by a windmill varies as the cube of the wind speed. In later years this enabled me to estimate from available wind records the rate of encroachment of sand dunes on oil fields in the Middle East.

I reported my results in two short papers published in the *Proceedings of the Royal Society* in 1936 and 1937. My book *The Physics of Blown Sand and Desert Dunes,* the first and only book covering the whole subject, was finished in 1939 at the start of the Second World

War. It was published in 1941 while I was abroad, by Methuen in England and by Morrow in the United States. Almost at once the book became, and has remained, the standard textbook on the subject for students of the earth sciences. It has run unchanged through a number of editions and is still in print.

Looking back, I am astonished that I managed to do so much in the five years from 1935 to 1939, and this in spite of interruptions, including three overseas expeditions that took me away for over a year, and in spite of being a complete novice at any kind of scientific research. I had two advantages. As an amateur with no academic background, my mind was uncluttered by any previous unproved and possibly misleading ideas. So I reasoned simply from the well-established principles of physics. Further, I had an almost unique field experience of the unimpeded behaviour of wind and sand in the entire absence of interference by rainfall or any living matter. I also had the ability to design and make my own bits of experimental equipment as I needed them, thus saving a lot of time.

Toward the end of 1934 I took a semiservice flat, 26A North Audley Street. The flat was ideal for what I wanted. Four of the other bachelor flats in the building were occupied by the sons of Lord Linlithgow, a former viceroy of India. Mine was the top-floor flat, well away from street noises. The flats were run efficiently by an excellent couple who did the housework and brought us each our breakfast. I usually lunched at Imperial College and dined at the Savile Club of Brook Street, to which I had been elected shortly after my move to North Audley Street. Stratton was a member of the club, and I already knew several others. It is a social club where one eats at a single long table and joins freely in the general talk. There was a billiard room, and I usually joined the group who frequented it for after-dinner snooker.

In the summer of 1935 I was asked by Surgeon Commander G. Murray-Levick, formerly doctor to the Shackleton Antarctic expedition, to be an assistant leader in his Public Schools Exploring

Society expedition to Newfoundland. It consisted of fifty school-boys and was very well run. I retain two impressions from the expedition: the primitive nature of the trackless interior of pine forests, and my astonishment that none of the boys had ever climbed a tree or had even wished to, whereas in my generation boys climbed trees instinctively.

At the end of 1935, when I was already immersed in the sand work at Imperial College, Stratton invited me to join his official Solar Eclipse Expedition to Japan in the following spring. He wanted a general handyman to look after the portable telescopes, coelostats, and other instruments, and, when the time came, to operate a telescope. I accepted at once, partly because I had had an invitation from Tommy Kirkpatrick to join him in what was then Tanganyika to climb Africa's highest mountain, Kilimanjaro. I could take a ship from Japan to Mombasa on my way home.

A total eclipse of the sun occurs anywhere in the world along a narrow strip of the earth's surface only a few times a century, and then only for a few minutes. Owing to the intense light from the disc itself, most of our knowledge of the sun's activity, chemical composition, and so on, can be gotten only when the disc itself is blotted out by the moon, leaving the corona alone visible as the ring of swirling, glowing material shoots out from the interior. Stratton was Britain's permanent eclipse observer, ready to lead an expedition anywhere the next path of totality happened to be. A set of special equipment was always kept ready.

In the early spring of 1936 we sailed with all the equipment in a Blue Funnel cargo ship that carried only half a dozen passengers as supernumeraries living with the ship's officers. We were a party of five, four astronomers and myself. Chubby Stratton's genius for keeping everyone happy and interested made the six-week voyage seem short and very enjoyable. Indeed, there was much to interest us. The ship had been designed for the Moslem pilgrim trade, according to government specifications. In the Red Sea we anchored off Jedda and took on a cargo of pilgrims returning from Mecca to the East. It was all perfectly organized. Each sect—Chinese, Indonesian, Malayan—had its own abbatoir, cookhouse, and so on, and a supply of live cattle.

Just before sailing, three very old gentlemen were carried aboard on stretchers. They were laid in a row on deck until quarters could be arranged for them. The ship gave the final three blasts of departure, whereupon all three died. They had no doubt been in the last stages of pneumonia. Thereafter, many of the pilgrims from the tropical regions also died of pneumonia contracted in the harsh, cold climate of Mecca. Most of them probably died happily, for the Pilgrimage was accomplished. There was nothing much else to live for. There were so many deaths on board that the ship ran out of firebars. It was a diesel ship, but firebars were stored for burial purposes.

Stratton had brought along double-elephant-size rolls of squared paper. Some of it was cut up into scoring cards for the "battleship" game, and the rest was used whole for drawing coastlines of imaginary islands for an elaborate yacht race game, each of which occupied many hours. On balmy tropical evenings under the cloudless Indian Ocean sky, we would watch for the sun to fall slowly into the sea. One of us would watch for the final moment when the last edge disappeared. The others, with their backs to the sun to avoid any chance of reversed aftersight, would immediately spring round to see a momentary bright green flash shoot up from where the sun had been. It interested the astronomers because there was no accepted explanation.

In Tokyo we stayed at the Imperial Hotel, a curious structure designed after the great earthquake to resist the next. We were met by an official party intent on seeing to our every need, and Stratton was welcomed by a large group of fellow astronomers. There followed a long train journey northward, across the strait to the north island of Hokkaido, and on to the island's capital, Sapporo. From there we were taken in official cars a long way farther north, the country getting wilder and wilder, to the tiny, remote village of

Kamishari on the northern coast. An iceberg was floating in the bay, and the Russian Kurile Islands could just be seen on the horizon.

We were housed with the village schoolmaster in a small but finely built wooden house with external walls of waterproof paper. For the first few days the schoolmaster spoke no word of English, leaving all communication to "honourable wife," who coped wonderfully. Then one morning he appeared speaking excellent English. He knew the language well, and had long taught it, but had never heard it spoken and so had no idea how it was pronounced. He had been quietly listening to us.

We soon got into the way of things, eating delicious home-cooked Japanese meals with chopsticks, alternately picking from an array of little dishes and shoveling in hot boiled rice from a personal bowl held close to one's chin. There was much raw fish, which we learned to relish. Honourable wife's father was the high priest of the temple at Namuro on the coast, and he sent us consignments of local oysters, each one seven inches across. One large bedroom had a bath in the centre, a wooden half-barrel with a charcoal stove in the middle round which one wrapped one's legs. Honourable wife would come to stoke the fire while we bathed. The floors of the house were bare wood, beautifully laid and immaculately polished. Wiser than we, no Japanese would dream of entering a private house with outdoor shoes on. A row of house slippers was kept in the front porch. The floors remained without a scratch. I once slipped and fell through the outside wall into six inches of snow. That was evidently common, for honourable wife immediately came carrying paper, brush, and a bucket of paste, patched up the hole, and gave the fire a little fanning, and we were as snug as if nothing had happened.

The village gentry, consisting of the schoolmaster, the doctor, the postmaster, and the policeman, would gather with us in the evenings, mainly I think to practice their English. They tried to teach us the game of Go, but the language barrier made it too difficult. Earlier in the evenings the village carpenter and bricklayer we employed would disappear after work, change into smart kimonos, and return for a cup of tea with us.

There are several active volcanos on Hokkaido, and hot springs abound. Most villages have a naturally heated bathing pool. Beside it, separately drained, is a shower that is always used before entering the pool. In the bath place everyone goes about entirely naked and unashamed. A visiting professor greeted us with "Let me introduce you to my wife." Both were naked.

Traveling through Hokkaido, we noticed a change in the features of many people. They looked less Oriental. Many had rosy cheeks. The men could grow quite reasonable beards, and some old women had big black mustaches tattooed on their upper lips. The island was formerly occupied by the Ainu people, a primitive tribe still in the hunting stage. Much interbreeding occurred as the Japanese pushed northward, and the remaining few pure Ainu are confined to one or two reservations. We were shown round one. They had many interesting customs. For instance, they catch a bear, keep it in a cage, feed it worshipfully for a year, and then eat it ceremonially.

There was much to do at our eclipse site. Brick emplacements had to be built for the telescopes and coelostats, and the instruments then had to be accurately aligned and adjusted. The telescopes were laid horizontally and fixed. The sun's rays were to be kept fixed on the telescope as it moved across the sky by means of a mirror which rotated on an axis parallel to the earth's. Each telescope thus had to have its own coelostat run by clockwork.

On the day of the eclipse, during May 1936, each of us had a telescope camera to operate—exposing, closing, and changing plates at certain preordained seconds. A total eclipse is a very strange occurrence. I remember two things before it became necessary to concentrate on my camera in the darkness. First, there was a huge wall of black night rushing toward us at a thousand miles an hour, blotting out hill after hill as it came. Then, as we saw the last vestige of the sun, a ring of isolated little stars—Bailly's beads—appeared, formed by the last light rays striking in between the mountains of the moon.

Once the eclipse was over and everything was packed up, we separated, each to see some different part of Japan on the main island of Honshu. I had been warned against the tourist hotels, which served ersatz Western food, doubtfully cooked. I stayed instead in Japanese-style hotels where everything was provided, from a toothbrush to a kimono to sleep in. Since eating in public was not done, meals were brought up to one's own room and put on a low table from which one ate while squatting on the floor.

I sailed from Yokohama for Mombasa in a small Japanese cargo ship, the only Westerner aboard. I noticed some sour faces, but fortunately realized the trouble. I hastened to tell the steward that I would prefer Japanese meals. He brightened at once, and so did the ship's officers. Knives and forks were put away. I enjoyed that long voyage to Africa. I taught the captain the battleship game, calling it the Battle of Tsushima, the Japanese Trafalgar where Admiral Togo defeated the Russian Grand Fleet in 1904.

Tommy Kirkpatrick was at that time director of the tropical agriculture research station at Amani, up in the hills in the ex-German territory of Tanganyika. The climate was ideal, although Amani was almost on the equator. His garden grew every kind of tropical fruit, including the *Monstera deliciosa,* whose enormous fruit really is delicious. On the road zigzagging upward we crossed and recrossed many times an endless, six-inch-wide column of ciafu, the highly organized nomad warrior ants. They wander, homeless, in tribes of countless millions. I was told they are apt to seize a village, strip it of everything edible, and then trek off elsewhere. The only possible escape was to get into a bath of water.

An important local crop, where the rain forest had been cleared, was a giant agave whose fibre was made into sisal. I was amused to watch a plant propagator in white overall and topee, looking small at the top of a tall ladder, with a tiny brush fertilizing an immense agave flower far bigger than himself.

We drove on to Moshi at the foot of Kilimanjaro. But no mountain could be seen, just a thin yellow haze in every direction. Then, looking upward at a seemingly impossible angle, I spotted a glint of sun on a piece of glacier, high up in the sky. The car took us up to the six-thousand-foot level, through native coffee fields beautifully kept and irrigated. There we collected the string of twenty porters that Tommy had organized, together with food supplies, and started upward into a perpetual fog under dripping trees of giant heather with yards of lichen hanging from their boughs. The fog persisted until we had reached nine thousand feet, where we emerged into bright sunlight. The heather was now more stunted, merely eight to ten feet tall. It was odd to see the porters ahead of us disappearing like little black dogs under waving heather blooms.

Everything here grew to a giant size. Even down at Amani the bamboo stalks were nine inches in diameter. Here on the mountain, six-foot stems of lobelia bore blue trumpet flowers two feet long. Stubby trees of groundsel had trunks a foot in diameter. As we rose further, the vegetation gradually shrank in size. The slopes resembled a huge Dartmoor with mansion-size blocks of old lava replacing granite tors. At fourteen thousand feet we reached the saddle between the two cones of Kibo and Mwenzi. Here the Germans had built a comfortable hut. We had previously decided to take five days for the whole ascent, to avoid the sickness and headaches others had complained of. We stayed a whole day at this hut, basking in the cool sunshine, before trudging up a steep ash slope to another old German hut at seventeen thousand feet. Leaving the porters there, the final hike to the crater lip at just under twenty thousand feet took us the whole next morning, walking slowly and breathlessly, the last bit through snow. From the rim we looked down into the great crater, five miles across and a thousand feet deep, with a mysterious black hole in the centre whose depth no one had then plumbed. A curious local legend persists that King Solomon tipped a vast treasure into that hole. Looking outward, we could see virtually nothing. The African plains and mountains were too far below. We and the mountain seemed isolated in space.

In the mid-nineteenth century when Hans Mayer first saw the crater of Kibo, it was filled to the brim with ice. Now, perhaps owing to some remaining volcanic activity, half of the crater is empty while the other half still contains an enormous block of ice. Tommy lifted one of the lava slabs on which we stood, and there, sure enough, was a Bible wrapped inside a waterproof box. For some odd reason, every Christian missionary feels it is his duty to plant the Word of God on Africa's highest mountain.

The process of acclimatization plays curious tricks. Even one hour at that great height was enough to readjust our machinery to the extent that we were able to run or slide straight down to the saddle hut more than five thousand feet below, and next morning to almost run up the opposite cone of Mwenzi, to nearly seventeen thousand feet. Long ago, in a single colossal explosion, Mwenzi blew itself in half, sideways. The whole of the north side disappeared, leaving a treacly-looking lava core like an enormous open drain channel standing upright. We crept up to a window in the semicircle of jagged pinnacles and looked down. According to previous reports, the void had always been filled by clouds so nothing could be seen. We were lucky. Perhaps for the first time any explorer had looked out, the void was cloudless. We looked vertically down a lava wall two miles deep. We could just distinguish individual groundsel trees growing at the bottom as pinheads. The African plains stretched outward indefinitely.

Later, Tommy drove me across the border into Kenya and I flew home from Nairobi, passing over the great lakes and herds of elephant and giraffe. There being then no high-flying jet aircraft, the scenery was clearly visible all the way.

Early in 1938 the wind-tunnel work had progressed to a stage at which the main results needed to be checked against the reality of true waterless desert conditions. This demanded a final expedition to the Egyptian-Libyan desert.

With the help of the Royal Geographical Society, I found a group of archaeologists anxious to trace, by its distinctive pottery, an ancient migration route from West Africa to the Nile. They also wanted to examine the rock painting in the Uweinat region of southwestern Egypt. During the expedition we had interesting discussions with this group of archaeologists. Their little party included an Armenian mechanic-photographer-handyman, a nice, friendly little man and a good and willing worker. In his youth he had been a "patriot," meaning a rebel activist against Turkish rule in reprisal for the atrocities inflicted on his people. He told lurid stories of his exploits, which included bank robbery and assassination. The Turkish atrocities had been horrible and had affected his own family in his own lifetime. This is in contrast with Ireland, where Cromwell's rough treatment of the Irish beyond the Pale happened three hundred years ago and was but a legend to the IRA.

My work necessitated waiting for a sand storm to blow up. To pass the waiting time, I had another aim, a bit of long-needed exploration. The drawback of motor transport is that it deters one from stopping, to post a letter, for example, and walking seems such a waste of time. On his eight-hundred-mile journey from Cairo to Uweinat, Prince Kemal el Din had skirted the eastern side of a seventy-mile-long horizon of high cliff. He mapped its main features from a distance and named it Gilf Kebir, or Great Cliff. Others after him, including myself, had also skirted this cliff. In 1932 Pat Clayton had rounded the southern extremity and found that the thousand-foot cliffs were continuous a long way up the western side of what must be a plateau half the size of Wales. As it seemed impossible to drive any kind of vehicle anywhere up that cliff, the plateau above had remained unexplored.

Our expedition reached the Gilf cliffs early in February 1938 and we camped halfway along its eastern side. The archaeologists started about their business, while my companion Ronald Peel and I, in a single car, drove north along the foot of the Gilf, farther than anyone had previously ventured. We came on a huge solitary sand drift that had spilled over from the plateau until its upper edge was level with the top. The sand surface was surprisingly firm as we walked up the crest of the drift. I also noticed a few rocks on it that

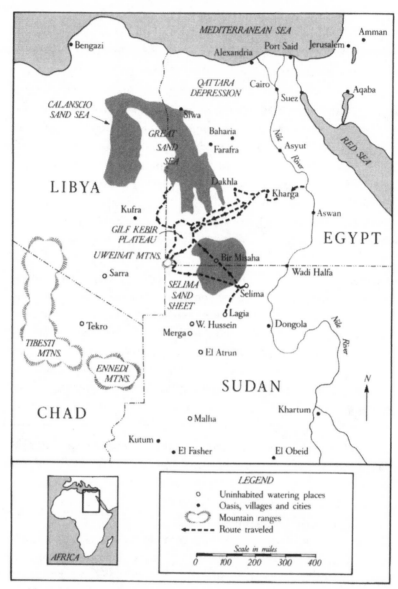

3. Map of the eastern Sahara showing the route of the 1938 expedition, Bagnold's last before World War II. Note that the Sarra Triangle has been ceded to Italy then occupying Libya (compare with maps 1 and 2).

were far too big to have been put there by the wind. Someone must have dropped them long ago. On our fourth attempt we succeeded in getting the car up the crest of the drift. We were on the hard rock of the plateau itself.

It seemed we had strayed into a secret Stone Age world. The top of our sand drift was signposted by a pair of tall cairns, neatly built by a professional. Our drift must have provided the only access long ago, just as it did now. A well-worn path led inland from the brink to successive factories of stone implements. Debris from the ancients' works lay strewn everywhere. It looked so fresh we half expected to come upon a group of uncouth artisans round the next corner. Yet we found no scrap of evidence that anyone had been here since prehistoric times. The endless booming of the wind against the great cliffs below increased the feeling of unreality and isolation.

After some weeks the rest of the party drove away to Kharga Oasis, some three hundred miles northeast, to get fresh food, more petrol, and water, and to wash. While they were away I spent an interesting eight days entirely alone. The only life, animal or vegetable, was a flock of migrating cranes which settled one night quite close by. I spent most of the time working up the results of my measurements and resetting instruments ready for the next sand storm. A heavy one blew up within a few days. I was well prepared for it, except, alas, I had lost my sand goggles. I spent some very uncomfortable hours sitting in the open, directly exposed to a violent sandblast, trying to keep my eyes open while taking readings from an array of gauges and sand traps. The purpose of eyelashes was very evident. Fortunately, I managed to get some reliable measurements which nicely confirmed my wind-tunnel measurements made in London.

One evening Peel and I found ourselves benighted quite far from camp. To shelter from the wind, I crawled into a crevice under a big slab of fallen caprock. Groping in the dark for somewhere to put my wristwatch for the night, my fingers found a little rock ledge.

On it was a stone knife. One of the Old People must have had the same idea very long ago.

On another occasion we were camped in the shelter of a big dune. Around midnight we were startled by a tremendous booming sound coming from the ground a few feet away; we could feel the sand vibrating beneath us. We had to shout to make ourselves heard. The dune had begun a spontaneous song. In the moonlight we saw an avalanche creeping slowly down the dune's slip face. The sound came from below, where the avalanche was slowing and the sand accumulating. I had often heard this "singing" in previous years, but now, after about a minute there came an answering boom, and then another, from dunes half a mile away. The vibrations from our dune must have started avalanches elsewhere. We had the eerie notion that these great beings were talking to one another in the stillness of the night.

Ralph Alger Bagnold, age seven, with his sister Enid, age thirteen.

Home on leave from the trenches, Ypres, Belgium, 1916.

With specially modified and outfitted Model-T Fords, we sallied forth into the Great Sand Sea in the autumn of 1929.

Flat out on the Great Selima Sand Sheet, 1930, with our Model-A Fords. Mud guards, bonnets [hoods], and doors have all been removed to reduce weight.

The 1930 expedition at Burg el Tuyur, a remote outcrop in the Great Selima Sand Sheet. Left to right are Captain V. C. Holland, W. B. Kennedy Shaw, Douglas Newbold, Lieutenant D. A. L. Dwyer, and Major R. A. Bagnold. Photograph by Lieutenant Guy L. Prendergast.

Upon discovering the Italians at Sarra Well in 1932, we dined in style as guests of Maggiori Lorenzini.

At Wadi Kutum we passed beyond the southern fringe of the Sahara.

Selima Oasis in northern Sudan is uninhabited and has long been a haven for desert expeditions.

Instead of dry sand, we stuck in mud kept wet by shallow groundwater at
Laqia Umran, northern Sudan, 1932.

Wind measurements being made with my multiple manometer in a sand storm near Gilf Kebir, 1938. The sand collector is in the middle ground. Photograph by Ronald Peel.

The early Long Range Desert Group patrols were manned by New Zealanders.

The earliest patrols of the Long Range Desert Group used 1939 Chevrolet trucks modified for desert operations. This patrol is crossing hazardous stony ground on the Harug el Aswad in Libya on the Murzuk raid, January 1941.

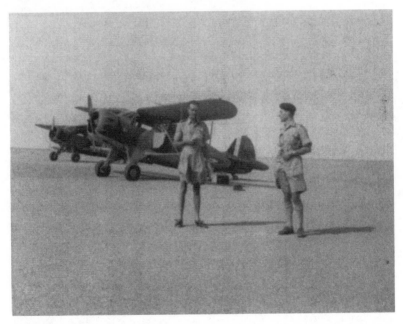

Two private Wacos made up the air arm of the LRDG. Here I confer with the French pilot, Lieutenant Mahé, of the Chad army, on serrir west of "Big Cairn," 1941.

Top. In 1956, Luna B. Leopold, then head of the Water Resources Division of the U.S. Geological Survey, and I took to one another from the start. *Above left.* In 1966, at age 70, I rafted the Colorado River through Cataract Canyon with Luna Leopold. It was one of the highlights of my life. Camping out in the open brought back many memories of old times. Photograph by Luna Leopold. *Above.* Plankie and me at Rickwoods, 1982. Photograph by Vance Haynes.

1 0

World War II
1939–1944

WITH THE OUTBREAK of war against Hitler's Germany in August 1939 I was recalled to the army as a reservist. I was posted to East Africa, I suppose to fill some vacancy. In September I sailed in a troopship that had been about to start on a luxury tour. It was provisioned accordingly, so we had unlimited caviare and other delicacies. The convoy steered a zigzag course through the Mediterranean to avoid submarines. The ship next to us must have mistaken starboard for port, for she ran straight into us at full speed. I was standing on deck and watched the crash. Our ship limped into Port Said, where we disembarked to wait for the next convoy.

I took this welcome opportunity to look up old friends in Cairo, and therefore caught the first available train. The next morning in Cairo, I was greeted by the then chief signal officer with "Just the man. Wavell wants to see you at once." "Wavell," I said, "what is such a top-ranking general doing out here?" "Hush," was the answer, "he's not supposed to be here. He's got a tiny office in an attic upstairs and is quietly planning something big. I'll take you up." I found a rather stocky man with a grim, weatherbeaten face, with one very bright eye. He evidently knew all about me and asked whether I would not rather serve in Egypt. I said that I most certainly would, and that was that. Within two days the War Office had changed my posting.

How had Wavell known I was in Cairo? Like him, I was not supposed to be in Egypt at all. Then I was shown a paragraph in the current *Egyptian Gazette* announcing the return of Major Bagnold to Egypt. The reporter must have spotted me the previous evening at the train station. His article went on to express gratification at this evidence that the War Office was at last trying to fit square pegs into square holes. How wrong he was.

I was sent to join the signal unit of the armored division at Mersa Matruh on the Mediterranean coast. The armored division itself was in first-class shape under General Hobart, a brilliant trainer of men and a leading advocate of mobility.

The situation in the autumn of 1939 was that Hitler had not yet begun any westward offensive and Mussolini had not yet declared war. It was hoped in London that he would never do so, and therefore no obvious warlike precautions against Italy were to be taken. BTE was still an independent command directly under the War Office. The troops in Palestine were similarly independent. Such tiny armed forces as existed for internal security in the Sudan, Somaliland, East Africa, and elsewhere were private armies under the orders of different government departments such as the Foreign Office or Colonial Office in London. There was no central policy regarding organization or equipment. Consequently, almost no knowledge existed in Cairo about the surrounding dependencies, nor, excepting the Sudan, was there any direct communication with them. The only fighting formation in Egypt was one incomplete and experimental armored division without transport to carry supplies of fuel more than a hundred miles, not far enough even to reach the boundary of its own defensive manor. Yet there was an imminent threat of an invasion in Egypt by the large Italian army in Libya, along the coastal strip between the Mediterranean and the great inland desert sands. There was also the threat of an invasion of the Sudan by another Italian army in Abyssinia. Each army was ten times the strength of what we had available. Moreover, although they were stationed in Egypt, our troops were neither trained nor equipped for real desert warfare, for Italy had never been considered a potential enemy.

There was another direction from which the Italian army in Libya might possibly threaten Egypt, the same vague menace from the interior that had kept so many defensive troops tied up during 1915–16. The menace then had been raiding parties of Senussi bedouin. Now it was the light, well-equipped columns of Italians, who could cross Egypt south of the sand sea to arrive without warning at Aswan or Wadi Halfa, cutting our communications with the Sudan. There would be nothing to stop them. I knew from experience that the six-hundred-mile journey from their outpost at Uweinat could be done in two days by a determined leader. I thought of Lorenzini. Suppose he were still in Libya?

I was shocked at the insular, peacetime attitude of the headquarters staff in Cairo under General Henry Maitland (Jumbo) Wilson and their total ignorance of the desert country beyond the Nile cultivation. In the general staff offices I could find but one small-scale map that extended westward to the Libyan border, and that showed little more detail than the Rohlfs expedition had brought back in 1874. The map faded out to the west with the inscription, "Limit of sand dunes unknown." I wrote a short note suggesting that we might at least buy a small assortment of desertworthy American vehicles and train a nucleus of officers and men in the art of cross-country driving, as the Light Car Patrols had been trained in 1916. I showed the note to General Hobart. "I entirely agree," he said, "I'll send this on to BTE, but I know what will happen. They'll turn it down." And so they did. General Hobart was removed, to everyone's dismay.

I showed my note to the new general, a man even more impatient with BTE's attitude, telling him what had happened before. He insisted on sending it again, and got an angry reply telling him it was none of his business. Shortly after that he asked me to take him round his manor, a defensive line stretching from the Mediterranean Sea to the Qattara Depression, a bottomless salt marsh. General Creagh, his chief staff officer, his aide-de-camp, and I had a pleasant three-day trip. I showed him the coastal plateau to within sight of the Italian forts, the Qattara Depression, the oasis of Siwa, and beyond it the northern rampart of the Great Sand Sea that barred all military operations for five hundred miles southward. On our return, the general found a furious message from BTE asking how he had dared to leave his headquarters. He laughed, "How does Jumbo think I can defend the frontier without having seen it?"

At the beginning of 1940 I was sent to Turkey with a small reconnaissance party, at the Turkish government's request. As a neutral country they were frightened of another German occupation, having had enough of that during the First World War. There had been talk of possible British help, and we were to explore this possibility. We were to dress in civilian clothes. An Indian tailor made me a suit within twenty-four hours, from the light material usual for Egypt. None of us bargained for the cold of the Anatolian Plateau. We found six inches of snow and a freezing wind. I was fortunate that I happened to possess a light overcoat.

The Turks were charming to us. They frankly answered all our questions about their military problems, but on the condition that we pass nothing on to the French. As aloof observers, they foresaw what was coming more clearly than we did. It was a strange experience to rub shoulders with German officers, also dressed as civilians, in the principal bar in Ankara, and to see obvious Gestapo men sitting at a corner table. On one occasion we traveled back from Adrianople to Constantinople in the same wagon-lit sleeping coach as the German ambassador von Papen.

Returning to Cairo, I found a great change. Wavell had emerged from his attic and had become an overlord, commander-in-chief Middle East, with responsibility for coordinating all British military actions over a quarter of the world, from Burma to South and West

Africa. A great new general headquarters (GHQ) was being created and staffed by new men just out from England, leaving the existing BTE headquarters intact but in a subordinate position. The heads of departments were mostly generals. My old friend R. E. Barker of our Irish days at the Curragh and in Maryborough Gaol arrived as General Barker, signal officer in chief. I became one of his staff. We had much work to do. Direct communications had to be created to link up the scattered and previously independent bits and pieces under one military command. Submarine cables had to be diverted to military use.

As time went on, an Italian invasion of Egypt along the coastal strip seemed ever more likely. At odd moments I pondered what use could be made of my almost unique knowledge of the desert and desert travel. A small, specially equipped force having an almost unheard-of range of self-contained action could surely do something useful. I remembered that curious meeting with Lorenzini nearly ten years earlier, and his dream of long-distance raiding. The appeasement policy had left us with no agents in Libya. We had no aircraft with sufficient range to go and see whether a base was being established at Uweinat, and we had no means of watching the southern part of the frontier on the ground.

Then came June 1940. The war exploded. Germany attacked the West; France was overrun and came under the rule of a puppet pro-German government at Vichy; Italy finally declared war in alliance with Germany. The Mediterranean became virtually closed to us, and the Middle East was isolated from England except by the long sea journey round the Cape of Good Hope or by dangerous high-flying aircraft. Marshall Graziani was already massing troops in eastern Libya. I felt I had to act. Digging out the third and last copy of the memo I had written half a year earlier, and which BTE had disdainfully rejected, I added a further, more definitive, paragraph. I asked the head of the operations section, whom I had known as a fellow cadet at Woolwich, to place it prominently on the commander in chief's desk. I felt rather as I had years ago when asking to see the chief of the Imperial General Staff. Here was I, a mere retired major from a technical corps, poking my nose into matters of defense policy at a critical wartime stage.

I was sent for within an hour. Wavell was alone. He waved me to an armchair and, picking up my memo, said quietly, "Tell me more about this." Knowing Wavell had served on Allenby's staff in Egypt during the last war, I mentioned the present lack of anything corresponding to the Light Car Patrols that would be able to give warning of possible attacks from the then unknown west. I told him briefly of the great range of action possible by small self-contained parties that had been especially trained and equipped. Such parties could operate anywhere in the uninhabited interior of Libya and could read tracks to find out if any offensive action against southern Egypt was in preparation. He seemed a bit skeptical and asked, "What would you do if you found no such preparations?" I said, "How about some piracy on the high desert?" At the word "piracy," his rather grim face suddenly broke into a broad grin. Without a moment's reflection he said, "Can you be ready in six weeks?" Taken aback, I said, "Yes Sir, provided . . ." He said, "Yes, of course. There'll be opposition and delay?" He pressed his bell, I thought for a clerk. Instead, a lieutenant general came in, Sir Arthur Smith, his chief of staff. "Arthur, Bagnold seeks a talisman. Get this typed out now, for my signature." He dictated, "To all heads of departments and branches. I wish any request by Major Bagnold in person to be granted immediately and without question." Then, turning to me he said, "When you are ready, write out your operation orders and bring them to me personally. I'll countersign them. Remember, not a word of this must get out. We are in a foreign country and there are sixty thousand enemy subjects going about freely. I can't stop them. Go to my DMI [Director of Military Intelligence] and get a good cover story."

I said, "There is the matter of volunteers." Wavell responded, "That's for General Wilson. I'll have a word with him first, and you'll find him very helpful."

I came away astounded. What a man! In an instant decision he had given me absolute carte blanche to do anything I thought best. There had been only two queries. How was I proposing to get into Libya? I told him, "Straight through the middle of the sand sea. It's safe because it's believed to be impassable." His other query had concerned the climate. Could white troops survive the summer temperatures and sand storms? I told him that was indeed a bit of a gamble, but the right sort of men could stand anything.

I wondered why my midget proposal should have been given such priority. Then I remembered that this man was the leading exponent of strategic deception. Faced with the probability of being attacked in overwhelming numbers, he was going to delay the enemy by bluff until he could get reinforcements from India and South Africa, if not from England. He would exploit the one great Italian weakness: the immense, undefended length of their single coastal supply road. At the same time, this would reawaken their old fear of attack from the unknown interior that had for thirty years confined them to the coastal strip. The small unit I proposed, with its extraordinary mobility and endurance, could create a threat out of proportion to reality, even though that mobility would greatly limit its firepower. We would be able to carry nothing heavier than machine guns and some land mines, both useless against walled forts. Wavell's response to my word "piracy" alone told me what he had in mind. It would be enough if we were to create the impression of British ubiquity throughout the interior of Libya.

I had to design, create, and train, within six weeks, a tiny private army of an entirely different kind from anything the military had considered practicable. Without that extraordinary talisman it would have been quite impossible. With it, I could press the right button on the great GHQ machine, and things would be done according to my specifications.

Three of the old hands of our former expedition days were available in the Middle East. I knew that Pat Clayton was surveying somewhere in Tanganyika. Bill Shaw was in Jerusalem as curator of the Palestine Museum. Rupert Harding-Newman was the Tank Corps representative in our advisory mission with the Egyptian army. Within forty-eight hours Clayton and Shaw were collected, commissioned as captains, and fitted out with uniforms. Harding-Newman could not leave his mission, but he gave us vital help during the first weeks.

I needed thirty sturdy American one-and-a-half-ton truck chassis on which ordinance workshops could build specially designed bodies. Rupert and I decided on two-wheel-drive commercial Chevrolets. All the agents in Egypt could together produce only fifteen. Rupert somehow managed to "borrow" the rest from the Egyptian army. We spent a day or so making working drawings of all the special modifications needed for the chassis and of all the other fittings required, for the workshops weren't to know what it was all for.

I then went to General Wilson at BTE. The commander in chief had clearly talked to him. They had both agreed that the New Zealanders would provide the best type of volunteer. The New Zealand division had arrived without its weaponry, which had been torpedoed at sea, and were consequently at loose ends. They should provide just the men I wanted—responsible, self-reliant sheep farmers, accustomed to great open spaces. Their commander, General Freyberg, was an imposing figure, a legendary veteran of the last war, having earned no less than three Victoria Crosses, and had been many times wounded. He grudgingly agreed to ask for volunteers, provided he could get special permission from his government for its nationals to serve under a foreign commander. That took several days. The answer came that the men could be "borrowed." Freyberg then sent a notice round asking for volunteers for "an important but dangerous mission." Half the division volunteered. He chose two of his officers to sort things out and pick 150 noncommissioned officers and enlisted men.

The New Zealanders were surely a little surprised to be met by what must have seemed three quite elderly leaders. I was forty-four,

Shaw was the same age but looked older. Clayton was indeed older and had prematurely white hair. However, enthusiasm mounted rapidly when the first of the trucks began to arrive from workshops and they learned what we planned to do and the strange sort of life it would entail. Even their army boots were to be discarded for open sandals. There was some opposition to discarding their traditional ANZAC felt hats, but that disappeared on the first outing in the open trucks when the hats all blew off in a cloud. Thereafter the Arab headdress was accepted, and even more so after the first strong wind when they found how well it protected their faces from sand-blast. For secrecy we had to get those headdresses from the Palestine police. I had the sandals made from a sample of the northwest frontier chapli worn by the tribesmen, the only kind of material tough enough to last.

A special ration scale had to be designed and authorized, suitable for small groups of men living in the open for weeks on end in the height of the summer heat and the chill of desert nights. I added a rum ration, abolished years before in all the fighting services. The director of medical services signed his agreement without a murmur, to the astonishment of the supply people, to whom ration scales were immutable.

Meanwhile, Bill Shaw took on the essential job of teaching the navigators the art of dead reckoning by compass, and of the astrofix by night with a theodolite and radio time signals. Navigating while on the move and being jolted over rock country required a number of special but simple devices I had evolved a decade before. All these had to be specified and obtained. I went through the Middle East stores of reserve equipment. The cupboard was almost bare. Having taken the machine guns and radio transmitters I needed, there remained only two guns and one radio. Fortunately, I knew the transmitters to be good ones. Designed to have a direct range of seventy miles, they had a skip range of over a thousand miles at certain hours of the day. General Barker let me have a bright young signal officer to take charge of communications and cyphers.

BTE gave us good barrack accommodations while the unit was forming. The commander in chief himself paid us one or two friendly visits. He arrived in a car flying two union jacks, with an appropriate escort of motorcycle outriders, pilot car in front, and a backup car with aides-de-camp and so forth. On one occasion the cortege turned up with War Secretary Anthony Eden (later, Churchill's successor as prime minister). Eden had an endearing charm with his seemingly indiscreet candid remarks, showing sound common sense, and his little human asides. Clayton, Shaw, and I had an office in general headquarters. John Shearer, the director of military intelligence, put us in with his active service counterpart in MI6. That was correct, really, though I didn't think of us as spies. I didn't care for that rather strange atmosphere and was glad when we later came directly under the Operations branch.

We were ready within the six weeks, with dumps of petrol, food, and water waiting at Siwa Oasis and at the far-off, uninhabited artesian spring at Dalla on the edge of the sands. I had asked Jumbo Wilson at his BTE headquarters for the loan of twenty three-ton lorries for help in making the Siwa dump. He made no difficulty and waved me off to his chief "Q" officer, a full colonel. I repeated the request, saying that I had come in the general's name. The colonel leaned back, aghast. "You ask for twenty lorries to go all the way to Siwa. They might easily get lost." Clayton, who was with me and still unused to army ways, blurted out, "My dear man, don't you realize that civilian buses go there twice a week?" We were both appalled at the persistent ignorance of Wilson's staff.

Wavell, complete with cortege, came to see us off and personally wish us good luck. One New Zealander was heard to say, "The old boy looks as if he's dying to come with us." Ten days later, on 13 September 1940, the patrols, each of forty men in ten trucks, gathered on a firm gravel plain on the Libyan side of the "impassable" sand barrier, having twice twisted our way through 150 miles of the giant dune field without seeing any solid ground. Two journeys had to be made to bring forward another load of petrol from the Dalla dump. I was pleased and rather astonished at being able to remember that tortuous route we had found ten years before, and still more so at the reaction of the New Zealanders. They had taken to the strange new life like ducks to water, quickly learning the tricky art of driving over dunes, spotting and avoiding the worst of the dry quicksands. We were fully self-contained for fourteen hundred miles more, being then six hundred miles from Cairo.

On 15 September 1940 we heard the broadcast news that the Italian army had crossed the Egyptian frontier. The invasion of Egypt had begun. (On that date twenty-four years earlier, during the Somme battle, tanks had been used for the first time and my division had captured two villages.) That same day, hundreds of miles farther south, our two tiny armed parties invaded Libya in the opposite direction. One patrol under Captain Teddy Mitford drove two hundred miles due west into enemy Libya, reading wheel tracks in the desert routes leading southward. There were no signs of enemy activity along them, so Mitford turned southward along the Italian "palificata," the signposted route to the oasis of Kufra two hundred miles away, which was held by a strong Italian garrison. Now in a piratical mood, Mitford's patrol burnt aviation spirit [fuel] stored by the Italians at emergency landing grounds and any unguarded aircraft they could find. Two heavy six-wheeled trucks carrying supplies and the official mail to Kufra were seized, together with their crews. As far as the Italians were concerned, the trucks "sunk without trace." Meanwhile, Clayton led another patrol southwest, passing just south of Kufra, to make contact with a French outpost on the edge of the Chad border, three hundred miles away. Again, no signs of enemy activity were found, though he had crossed Libya from side to side.

The whole party rendezvoused at the southern tip of the Gilf Kebir where I had arranged another supply dump. We returned to Cairo via Kharga Oasis. We had covered four thousand miles, half of that through enemy country, and the venture had been a success. It demonstrated beyond doubt the capability of small armed groups

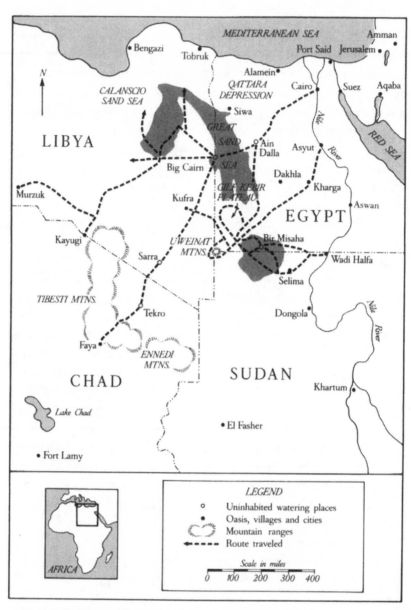

4. Map of the Western Desert showing operational routes of the Long Range Desert Group, 1940–41.

to travel anywhere in the interior of Libya. It had falsified the traditional military tenet that a great desert constituted a secure defensive flank.

With that success, Wavell ordered the number of patrols to be doubled. Volunteers for each new patrol were drawn from a different regiment or group—Guards, Rhodesians, Yeomanry, Indians, and so on. The unit was officially named the Long Range Desert Group (LRDG) and came directly under Operations. I became an acting lieutenant colonel.

During the next few months, raids were made on a number of enemy-held oases. For greater effect, isolated little garrisons hundreds of miles apart were shot up, when possible on the same day. To the Italians, the raiders seemed to appear from nowhere, as if from a fourth dimension, and to disappear just as rapidly. The British seemed to be everywhere. Based on the radio intercepts, Graziani was beginning to doubt his intelligence reports of our weakness. The invading Italian army halted for vital months.

By the end of November, Clayton, Shaw, and I, the planners, were beginning to run out of convenient little targets in eastern Libya. The Murzuk group of oases in the far southwest of Libya, near the border with Algeria, looked very tempting. Far from the active war zone, the garrisons there were sure to be asleep. But Murzuk was far beyond our range. A total journey of over three thousand miles would be required. It might be possible, though, if we could get further supplies from the French army in Chad province. Unfortunately, no one in general headquarters seemed to know which side the Chad province was on. All the other French overseas possessions were loyal to the pro-German Vichy government.

Shaw suggested that the best source of information was Douglas Newbold, since he was now political head of the Sudan government, Chad's next-door neighbour. So I flew to Khartoum and spent an evening with Douglas. Yes, he knew the governor of Chad, a shrewd little Negro from Martinique named Eboué. Douglas thought Eboué would like to come in on our side, but there was dissension. The army commander was pro-Vichy, while the younger officers wanted to join the Allies. Another problem was that if the province did actively join the Allies, it might be attacked by the strongly pro-Vichy Niger province. "I'm afraid my hands are tied," Douglas said. "Negotiations with French overseas provinces are top-level Churchill–de Gaulle stuff. But you've got no diplomatic status. Why don't you fly across and see them at Fort Lamy (now Njamina)? I'll arrange a flight for you."

The next morning I drove to the simple airfield at Gordon's Tree and found that I had a BOAC airliner to myself. I was about to board when a car drove up in a cloud of dust. It was Anthony Eden again. "Awfully sorry, old boy. The Boss has sent for me urgently. It's as much as my job's worth to keep the Boss waiting. I'll have to steal your aircraft." Off he went to Cairo. However, Douglas quickly conjured up another aircraft, and I flew halfway across Africa to Fort Lamy. On arriving, I suddenly collapsed on the tarmac due to a violent fever I used to get occasionally, possibly an aftermath of malaria.

The aircraft must have carried an unofficial note of introduction from Douglas Newbold, for I regained consciousness in a tastefully furnished bedroom nursed by a charming Negro lady, the governor's wife. A few hours later there followed a strange bedside conference in French. The governor entered with a tall, fair-haired lieutenant colonel in flowing mehariste uniform, whom he introduced as d'Ornano, the army second in command. A Corsican, he added, to explain the name. D'Ornano peered round. "He's not here?" "No," said Eboué. "He refuses to take any part in this." "Good," said d'Ornano. "Then I will speak for the army." Then, turning to me, "Were those your people who came and scared the wits out of my outpost at Tekro? And they had driven all the way from Cairo? *Tiens.* But you haven't come here for nothing. What do you want?"

I told them quite frankly about the planned raid on Murzuk, and handed d'Ornano a list of the extra supplies we would need: petrol, water, and some French army rations. They looked at one another, and d'Ornano said to the governor, "This is IT. We've got to decide NOW." Thumping the table, "This is our chance. My officers are getting restive. I can't hold them inactive much longer. You agree?" The governor nodded. Then d'Ornano turned to me. "I'll do all you ask, but on one condition. You take me with you to Murzuk, and one of my officers, and we fly the French flag alongside yours."

They were ready to burn their boats, ignoring their commander and the threat of attack from Niger. The unexpected participation of the Free French would greatly increase the psychological effect on the enemy. I agreed at once. We fixed a date and a rendezvous north of the Tibesti Mountains, close to the Libyan border. D'Ornano then and there produced a sheet of paper and wrote out a formal contract between Lieutenant Colonel Bagnold and the French army of Chad. We both signed it in the governor's presence.

Everything went according to plan. The dune fields were oriented in the right direction, so although there were no maps, Clayton's two patrols arrived at the rendezvous after their thousand-mile journey and duly joined d'Ornano and Capitaine Massu (Massu afterward became commander in chief of the French army in Algeria). The combined raid on the Murzuk oases was highly successful, though sadly, d'Ornano received a fatal bullet. He must have been almost the first Free French casualty in action against the Axis powers. He was a Frenchman in the very best tradition.

My unorthodox journey to Chad, made with Newbold's discreet connivance, had two immediate consequences. Chad came in openly and voluntarily on the Allied side, the only French overseas dependency to do so. This allowed de Gaulle, then fighting to establish his rule farther south in Gabon, to send Colonel Leclerc to Chad as military commander. Leclerc immediately started improvising a force for his daring and successful expedition across the desert to capture Kufra from the Italians. Its garrison had been too strong for us to tackle. Leclerc's force included a field gun, which our light and mobile LRDG did not have. It did the trick. Its shells holed the fort walls and the garrison surrendered. Documents captured at Kufra made it clear that the Italians had never bothered before the war to buy the Egyptian maps on which Clayton had drawn our route across the sand sea. They never discovered our secret passage into inner Libya.

Leclerc was a professional soldier who later became famous as the general whose armored division liberated Paris. His real name was Philippe de Hautclocque. He escaped from France in 1940 under the assumed name of Leclerc, which he chose to retain. He was an inspiring leader and a brilliant organizer. We became friends and helped each other in various small ways.

In order to bolster de Gaulle's movement, it was given out from London that the Murzuk operation had been a purely French enterprise, whereas in fact I had conceived and organized the whole thing with the help of d'Ornano. In the long run, though, the deception was for the best.

On the return journey from Murzuk the LRDG patrols were to cooperate with Leclerc's Kufra expedition. That may have been a mistake, for our patrols had already traveled well over two thousand miles, most of it across unknown and unmapped country. Near Kufra, one patrol was spotted by an Italian aircraft and destroyed. Clayton himself was captured and spent the rest of the war as a prisoner.

After Leclerc's siege and capture of Kufra, logistics forced him to leave one native battalion there, living on Italian rations. The whole oasis group consequently became a liability. It had not only to be defended, but also to be kept supplied from the Nile Valley, seven hundred miles away across the desert. An immense convoy operation had to be organized. The round trip, with the available three-ton lorries, took between two and three weeks. The LRDG being the only unit capable of getting there quickly, we were moved to Kufra. I became the military governor of the whole oasis group, nominally an official of the "Occupied Enemy Territory Administration" (OETA). To get some sense of scale, imagine northern Europe as an empty, rainless desert of sand and rock, with London as the main oasis a few miles across, watered from shallow artesian wells, with palm groves, villages, salt lakes, and an Arab population of four thousand. Then, the suburb of Taiserbo, with another thousand Arabs, would lie northwest where Liverpool is, with one uninhabited water hole between, near Derby. Ribiana, with five hundred more people, would lie near Bristol, cut off by a sea of dunes. On the same scale, Cairo would be at Copenhagen, across a waterless "North Sea" full of great dune fields. Wadi Halfa on the Nile would lie near Munich. Nothing but desert lay between.

Meanwhile, Wavell had brought off his great coup. His brilliant field commander, General Dick O'Connor, captured the whole of Graziani's army on the coast. By the end of March 1941, however, Rommel and his Afrika Corps had arrived. The enemy was almost at the Egyptian frontier, and Dick O'Connor had been captured.

Shortly before the LRDG was moved out to Kufra, I got a message that General de Gaulle was asking to see me. Like a good Frenchman, he refused to speak anything but French. Whereas the English tend to speak English loudly to foreigners, de Gaulle spoke in French painfully slowly. I followed him with some difficulty. I got the impression of a great man carrying the whole French nation embodied in himself. He seemed almost to be using the royal "we." He wanted to impress on me that since Kufra had been captured by France, it was to be considered as French until a peace treaty decided otherwise. Hence I must fly the French flag alongside the British. As leader of the new French, he clearly needed to reestablish every possible scrap of French international rights. The French people were then in a terrible dilemma. As Leclerc had put it to me, "The French are a proud people. They are now realizing they have made a ghastly mistake."

The whole unit drove to Kufra across the sand sea in the April heat. Before the war, desert expeditions had been confined to the winter months. No one could be found who had personal experience of the summer heat in the desert interior. Some years previously, three German explorers had disappeared, believed to have been overwhelmed in a sandstorm. Indeed, legends of such disasters went back to the fifth century B.C. During our move, temperatures exceeding 50°C (120°F) were found to be tolerable, even on a restricted water ration, owing to the dryness. The worst discomfort came from severe sandstorms which lasted several days. They made eating very difficult.

We settled down in Kufra for the summer, along with the French. It was a tantalizing situation. Kufra was ideally situated to be a base (which it later became) from which we could have reconnoitered and raided northward against the long German supply line from Tripoli. But we were immobilized by lack of petrol.

Kufra was a little kingdom in the variety of its affairs. There was practically no grazing, for the last effective rain had fallen some seventy years before, so meat was very scarce. The oasis had formerly been an entrepôt for trade caravans from Equatorial Africa to the coast. The war had stopped all that. To restart some trade, I sent the chief merchant to the Nile with the first returning supply convoy, giving him credit to buy goods for sale or barter. At the same time, I asked the French in Chad to spread the news around the Tibesti region. Presently a flock of fat-tailed sheep arrived on the hoof, having been driven over two hundred miles of waterless desert with but a single water hole. The New Zealanders had never seen fat-tailed sheep before and argued about what they might be. A currency difficulty then had to be sorted out. The French franc and the Italian lira had no known local values. OETA had decreed that neither could have any value, but the inhabitants had to live. So I laid down a common arbitrary exchange value.

Communication with Cairo was a serious problem. I needed to keep in touch with what was going on. Radio was ruled out, except in an emergency, and the cross-country journey took at least three days. By good fortune, Guy Prendergast arrived from England about that time. I had tried for some months to get him flown out as my second in command. With his long experience of private flying, he saw the solution at once. The RAF had previously refused to allow another fighting service to use their aircraft. In defiance, we bought two light aircraft from an Egyptian pasha. They were tiny single-engined machines, and when fitted out for desert work they had a range of only three hundred miles. However, by establishing intermediate petrol dumps and taking some risks, especially when crossing the sand sea in the summer heat, we were just able to do the journey to Cairo in a day. Our truck navigators soon became expert in the air as well, and we used to make quite hair-raising journeys when every ground feature had disappeared in the hot haze of a storm. Prendergast himself was an experienced pilot. We discovered another among the New Zealanders, and for a time I borrowed a young French army pilot from Chad. The RAF refused to service our little machines, but the Egyptian mechanics at the Cairo civil airport kept them in excellent condition.

In the end, it became obvious that one of us would have to be back at general headquarters all the time. In July I handed over command of the LRDG to Prendergast and put on a red hat in Cairo as a full colonel. There was another consideration. At forty-five, after prolonged rough living in the intense heat, I was no longer feeling my best. I suspected that my adrenal gland had been over-taxed.

I think that the best summary of the LRDG's early activities was the one written by the commander in chief himself in his official dispatch of October 1941. The following extract was very kindly given to me in advance by General Wavell:

> I would like to take this opportunity to bring to notice a small body of men who have for a year past done inconspicuous but invaluable service, the Long Range Desert Group. It was formed under Major (now Colonel) R. A. Bagnold in July 1940 to reconnoitre the great Libyan Desert on the western border of Egypt and the Sudan. Operating in small independent columns, the group has penetrated into nearly every part of the desert Libya, an area comparable in size with that of India.

Not only have the patrols brought back much information, but they have attacked enemy forts, captured personnel [and] transport and grounded aircraft as far as 800 miles inside hostile territory. They have protected Egypt and the Sudan from any possibility of raids, and have caused the enemy, in lively apprehension of their activities, to tie up considerable forces in the defense of distant outposts. Their journeys across vast regions of unexplored desert have entailed the crossing of physical obstacles and the endurance of extreme summer temperatures, both of which would, a year ago, have been deemed impossible. Their exploits have been achieved only by careful organization and a very high standard of enterprise, discipline, mechanical maintenance and desert navigation. The personnel of these patrols was originally drawn almost entirely from the New Zealand forces; later officers and men from British units and from Southern Rhodesia joined the group. A special word of praise must be added for the R.A.O.C. fitters whose work contributed so much to the mechanical endurance of the vehicles in such unprecedented conditions.

A. P. Wavell

Anthony Eden mentioned to me that Wavell referred to us in private as his "mosquito army." There were never more than two hundred of us. The army proper could not understand how we got about or how we kept ourselves supplied. In looking back, it is strange that Wavell never told me what to do. I got no definite orders. The three of us—the old hands—made our own plans.

So great had the reputation and mystery of the Long Range Desert Group become that the BTE staff in Cairo became jocularly known as the Short Range Shepheards Group, the veranda and bar of Shepheards Hotel being a traditional evening meetingplace for British residents.

Among the LRDG's subsequent activities there may be mentioned a close liaison with another "private army," David Stirling's SAS (Special Air Service). Trained to parachute in and destroy enemy aircraft with sticky bombs, the SAS had found that the RAF in the Middle East had no suitable aircraft to carry them. So, by a mutual arrangement, the LRDG provided ground transport instead, navigating them to within walking distance of enemy airfields under cover of darkness. Eventually the SAS got transport of their own.

Perhaps the LRDG's most astonishing achievement was the undetected maintenance for eighteen months of a well-camouflaged observation post beside a lonely stretch of coastal road far inside enemy territory. That post was able to record and report by radio every troop and transport movement to and from the enemy's front.

Among other things, the LRDG contributed to the mapping of the interior desert. After each patrol the navigator would hand in his route plot and notes to Shaw, who served as our intelligence officer. In this way, information gradually accumulated from which new maps could be drawn on a uniform system of representation, which the often imaginary Italian maps lacked. The absence of a comprehensive small-scale map of northeast Africa as a whole was perhaps one of the reasons, apart from security, why the LRDG and its movements remained so much an enigma to the rest of the army. The topographical aspect of the LRDG's work was later developed still further by the addition of its own survey section.

Ultimately, I returned to signals on appointment as deputy signal officer in chief with the rank of brigadier. Toward the end of the North African campaign, after my general had been recalled to England, I was left to do his job. During that time, one or two rather curious incidents occurred.

Just before Hitler's invasion of Russia, a revived threat arose of a German thrust through Turkey. Better communications with that country from Cairo were clearly needed. The long and aged single-wire telegraph line across Sinai and along the whole of the Levant was to be replaced by a modern multichannel system from Cairo to Ankara. It was known that the Germans were already installing such a system from the Balkans toward Ankara, so there was some urgency. It is not easy to adjust to the difference in outlook between a neutral and a belligerent nation. Both sides applied to the Turkish PTT for office space to install their somewhat elaborate terminal

equipment. The Turks, tongues in cheeks, allotted the same room
to both English and Germans. It must have tickled their sense of
humor. From the long-term peacetime view, this was perfectly
sound. The mutually hostile parties eventually took to borrowing
each other's screwdrivers.

I mentioned to the minister that we should like to place a large
order for trees suitable for telegraph poles. He said, "Certainly, we
can include such an order next year when the budget is considered."
The transaction was, however, quickly arranged through the right
channels, no doubt with the aid of a fixer.

I had taken a young officer with me to Turkey. He was a Roman
history don at Oxford, and at Ankara he showed me the only existing copy of the Acts of Augustus, inscribed on a rock face. We had
identical hotel rooms in Ankara. When paying the bill, I noticed
that my room cost twice as much as his. On querying this, it was
explained that my room was guaranteed free of bedbugs, but his
was not.

The four Allied rulers planned to confer in Cairo. The beautiful
old Mena Hotel just below the Giza pyramids was commandeered
and all the inmates evacuated. Every one of the wealthy owners of
the villas along the avenue from the city was heavily bribed to va-
cate. Ramps were placed everywhere Roosevelt might want to
move in a wheelchair. We created a special signal office to handle
international traffic, with relays of dispatch riders and multilingual
telephone operators. For security against possible German bombing, a heavy concentration of antiaircraft batteries was collected
(under Brigadier Sir Mortimer Wheeler, the archaeologist). At the
last moment, the Four decided to confer instead in Teheran, and the
great Cairo Conference never was.

I got to know the late Walter Emery, a well-known Egyptologist
who specialized in the Archaic Period of the first and second dynasties, about which little is known because of the lack of inscriptions.
He was a tall, thin man, often to be found coiled up in a Turf Club
armchair with a glass of beer. One day he took me to Saqqara to

see his latest find. The tombs of the first-dynasty pharaohs were thought to have been destroyed during the civil war in the second dynasty. However, Emery had a genius for estimating where they should lie, and he had already discovered more than one. Now he had found the tomb site of a first-dynasty pharaoh named by the primitive hieroglyphics as Hor Aha. He was either Menes himself, the founder of all the dynasties, or his immediate successor.

The actual tomb chamber had been burned, but beside it, intact, was a storeroom containing the things Hor Aha was most likely to need in the hereafter. There was a dinner service of modern shape, carved so thinly from alabaster rock that the plates were almost transparent. More extraordinary, Hor Aha must in his private life have been a DIY (do-it-yourself) man with cabinetmaking as his hobby, for there was a finely finished tool chest, packed ready for use and still as sound as when it was made. It was metalbound with a tray on top, just like a schoolboy's playbox. In the tray lay a set of bronze chisels of quite modern design, wood handled and metal ferruled. Below lay a mallet, a bronze saw, and the other expected tools. The saw was still sharp; I cut through a piece of wood with it.

Here, at the first misty dawn of recorded history, five thousand years ago, was a well-developed civilization. Where did it come from? Did the invading Horus people bring it from across the Indian Ocean, or was it indigenous? To me, that was one of the most thrilling days of the war.

My father died early in 1944, in his ninetieth year, after a succession of strokes. As the North African campaign was over, I applied for and was granted release from further army service in order to settle his affairs. Warren Wood, the family home for the last forty years, was in a dangerous position, being less than two miles from Woolwich Arsenal. The German "doodle-bugs" were starting to rain on London. I flew home in April in an RAF bomber, a two-day journey via Lisbon. As was customary, having put on full flying clothes to ensure against the cold, I took a "knock-out" pill and knew nothing of the journey.

On my return to England, I wrote the following letter to Wavell, then viceroy of India:

Dear Lord Wavell

My father died not long ago. On going through his papers I came across the enclosed (top half). In view of the sequel, the original of which I naturally treasure, it makes a strange coincidence.

Who was Colonel A. H. Wavell? Possibly an uncle of yours? I would be most interested to know.

Yours sincerely

R. A. B.

The following is the letter I had found in my father's papers:

GENERAL ORDERS

Pietermaritsburg
January 14 1881

Congratulations

The Major General commanding desires to record his high sense of the energy shown by Lieutenant Bagnold and the officers and men of the Telegraph Troop R.E. in carrying out a duty of a specially arduous nature under very adverse conditions, and he considers this officer and those under his command are deserving of great praise for the zeal and ability displayed.

By Order
A. H. Wavell, Colonel
For the Chief of Staff

The "sequel" I received fifty-nine years later is:

General Headquarters Middle East
Cairo 1st October 1940

Dear Bagnold

I should like to convey to the officers and other ranks under your command my congratulations and appreciation of the successful results of the recent patrols carried out by your unit in central Libya.

I am aware of the extreme physical difficulties which had to be overcome, particularly the intense heat.

That your operation, involving as it did 150,000 truck-miles, has been brought to a successful conclusion indicates a high standard of efficiency in preparation and execution of which you, your officers and men may justly be proud.

Yours sincerely

A. P. Wavell

Wavell wrote back:

The Viceroy's House
New Delhi

Dear Bagnold

Many thanks for your letter of January 28. I am very glad to hear from you again. Curiously enough, I had been talking about you and your desert patrols only a short time before with Dick O'Connor. He is now commanding the Eastern Army at Calcutta and is in very good heart in spite of his three years captivity; he made three attempts to escape, and got away the third time.

The A. H. Wavell of the extract you sent me was my uncle, my father's eldest brother. He was in the 41st Regiment and then went on the staff. He died in 1891 and I never knew him. You may have known his eldest son, my cousin Arthur Wavell, who went to Mecca and wrote "A Modern Pilgrimage to Mecca." The two extracts you sent make an interesting coincidence.

I hope you are well and prospering. With all best wishes

Wavell

11

Lyminge—Marriage—Shell
1944–1949

ON MY RETURN to England I was astonished to find that I had been elected a Fellow of the Royal Society. I had had no inkling that I had been proposed or even considered. Thus my vague wish as a young officer to become an FRS rather than a general had come true. It was more surprising because I was merely an amateur scientist with no academic standing.

I had retained my top-floor flat in North Audley Street, London, and it had been kept in good order during my five-year absence. I took my meals as before at the Savile Club, close by in Brook Street. The bombardment of London by flying bombs (buzz bombs) was in full swing. From my bedroom the sound of their approach was almost indistinguishable from that of a bus starting up in the street below. The bomb fell as soon as its engine stopped. If the noise continued overhead, one was safe. If it stopped, there was no time to dash down four flights of stairs, and the lift would probably be already occupied, so I just stayed in bed. Fortunately, most of the West End remained relatively undamaged.

My first task was to dispose of Warren Wood, which was now empty. At the same time I had to buy a house in which to keep the furniture and other belongings. I wanted a house somewhere in the southeast, close to London but in an area of low bombing. I finally found a suitable little house at Lyminge near Folkestone, outside the balloon barrage. (Being one of the main targets of bombing, London was surrounded by a ring of captive balloons. Their anchor wires brought down many enemy night bombers.)

Plans were being made for a massive landing somewhere on the Channel coast. I was asked to undertake research on the action of sea waves on the formation or erosion of beaches, sponsored by Mountbatten's Combined Operations Directorate. A part of the hydraulics laboratory at Imperial College was available under my old friend John Francis, who had taken Professor White's place. The big wave tank I had built before the war for the wave-pressure work was still there, together with much other apparatus. I lived at the North Audley Street flat during the week and spent the weekends at Lyminge where, in my own workshop, I designed and made most of the measuring instruments I would need.

On the strictly practical side, engineers had long striven to build coastal defenses against the sea, while on the theoretical side, mathematicians had devised satisfactory models of wave motions under ideal conditions. But these excluded the reality of waves dissipating their energy against a beach. The real physical processes whereby shallow-water waves transport sand and shingle from place to place were still unexplored and considered beyond the scope of reliable theory. I found it possible to discover a lot about the general physical processes involved by undertaking well-designed experiments. Some years later, working with Douglas Inman at the Scripps Institution of Oceanography in La Jolla, California, I was able to follow up the laboratory experiments by directly seeing the effects of wave motions on the seabed. Using a snorkel, I could lie close to the bottom and drift to and fro under the long Pacific swells, watching plumes of sand being tossed upward by water vortices created at the end of each wave oscillation.

Since my return to England I found myself closer than before to my sister Enid. I had always been welcome at her house, but the six-

and-a-half-year age difference had long kept us apart. I had always been "my little brother" to her. We had different interests. Hers were literary and social. She had made a name for herself as an authoress and playwright. She had married Sir Roderick Jones, the owner and autocratic chairman of Reuters, the worldwide news agency. She had a full life bringing up her four children, writing, and managing three big houses with a commuting indoor staff of ten or more. One house was in London, at 29 Hyde Park Gate, another was Northend House at Rottingdean in Sussex, and the third was Kipling's former estate. In the early days, Kipling was still living there and would sometimes drop in for tea. I remember him as a thin old man with heavy, projecting black eyebrows.

Enid and I had two things in common—fond memories of our early childhood days in Jamaica and a disregard for convention which in our different ways amounted to a practical inventiveness. If something seemed useful to be done, we did it, even though it had never been done or thought of before. As an example, Enid wanted fresh milk for her children, something difficult to get in wartime London. She took her Guernsey cow, Daisy, from Rottingdean to Hyde Park Gate and stabled her in one of the garages. Daisy grazed happily in the royal parkland just across the Piccadilly-Kensington thoroughfare. Every morning and evening the police held up the traffic for Daisy to cross: "Make way for Lady Jones's cow." Much the same order was given when Churchill drove out from No. 28 next door. The police were merely amused. One after another, the various authorities sent inspectors but could find nothing to forbid. And no one objected to Daisy's modest little pats.

It was at Enid's that I came to know Dorothy Plank, a friend of the family and originally called "Plankie" by the children. The name stuck. Plankie and I were married in the little Rottingdean church. The bride was given away by my brother-in- law, Roderick. We spent our honeymoon in Eire, at a hotel in Dun Laoghaire (formerly Kingstown) on Dublin Bay. The free-and-easy atmosphere of a neutral country was refreshing after the wartime austerity at home. The shops were full of things impossible to get in England.

Clothing was still rationed in Eire, but the hotel told us simply to ask our chambermaid for as many coupons as we wanted.

Part of a restaurant near our hotel was devoted to fruit machines (slot machines) and pin tables. We once saw a priest come in leading a string of small children, who immediately set to work on the fruit machines. After awhile, the priest gathered them up. "There y'are, y'see. Y've lost y'r money, as I told y'." Sound, practical religion.

On the eve of our departure from Ireland, we saw for sale a magnificent whole ham such as had not been seen in England since before the war. We were told that the export of fresh meat was forbidden. When we asked at the local police station to verify this, a kindly lieutenant said, "Yes, it's illegal. But wait now while I think. I have a cousin in the customs at Holyhead . . ." The ham accompanied us on our return to England, but only after some initial delays. On the flight home we had to return to Dublin because someone had forgotten to replace the lid of a fuel tank and the fuel was streaming away.

The little house at Lyminge suited us very well. Together with three other small properties, it formed part of an isolated colony on the heights a few miles west of Folkestone. The village of Lyminge itself lay inland from our colony but within walking distance. On a clear day one could see the coast of France in the far distance, viewed across a field of beans. A neighbor kept a small herd of Jersey cows, so we were able to make real Devonshire cream.

The following year, 1947, out of the blue, John Oriel called with the offer of a job as director of research in his Shell Refining and Marketing Company, a subsidiary of the international Shell Group and responsible for operations in the United Kingdom. It would be entirely out of my line, for I never had any connections with the oil industry except for the friendly help we had received from the Shell Company of Egypt. I have never understood quite why I was picked for such a job. However, I took an immediate liking to John Oriel, and the position, salary, and perks were so attractive that I decided to have a go, even though it meant selling our little house in Lyminge and moving to Cheshire.

The international Anglo-Dutch Shell Group controls national companies in nearly every country in the world, including the major Shell Oil Company of America. The Dutch and American sides each have well-established research centres, in Amsterdam and California, respectively. In addition, research groups had sprung up in the United Kingdom, and it had been decided to amalgamate these to form a third research centre at Thornton, close to the Shell refinery at Stanlow in Cheshire. Shell moved us most efficiently to Abbots Bank, a fine house Oriel had bought for us on Westminster Avenue on the outskirts of Chester.

It was decided that I should start with visits to Holland and the United States to get to know something of Shell and its people. The first thing I noticed on arrival by sea at Hook of Holland was that instead of the usual two customs control entrances, there were three—one for nationals, another for aliens, and a third for Shell. The large research centre in Amsterdam was run, unusually, by two coequal directors, one for the research proper, the other to do all the administrative work. It was an ideal system that appeared to work admirably, and which university professors would envy. However, it undoubtedly depended very much on a lucky choice of personalities.

Shortly afterward, I flew to New York on the Dutch airline, KLM. This was the early days of transatlantic crossings, and we spent a night in the Azores. In true Dutch form, every two to three hours during the flight they served long, heavy meals. After a few days in New York with the Shell Oil management, I took a three-day train journey across America to the West Coast. My chats with fellow passengers gave me the impression that being in the oil business made one something of an aristocrat.

After a somewhat strenuous tour I returned to England on the *Queen Elizabeth I*; I had been given a cabin on the VIP deck. I was astonished to find a uniformed Russian officer armed with a revolver standing between my door and the next. He woodenly let me pass. Then I remembered that the United Nations Security Council had been meeting in New York and assumed that my neighbor was a diplomat. It took me most of the voyage to explore that great ship. On the fourth day, after climbing numerous stairways, I came upon a small, isolated deck. It was deserted except for two deck chairs in the far corner, side by side, containing the foreign ministers of Great Britain and Soviet Russia. They were all alone, asleep.

We liked Chester. It was then a quiet cathedral city, unspoilt by the traffic that now chokes it. Plankie enjoyed the friendly shops, many of which still held stocks of prewar goods. Our son Stephen was born in Chester, delivered by our doctor, Dobie, who had been a student with me at Caius. Stephen was christened in the cathedral by the bishop, who was also an old Caius man. Stephen was an enterprising baby. At the christening he reached up and pulled the bishop's glasses off. John Oriel stood as godfather. We made many friends, both within the Shell family and outside. I was selected to be on the Council of Liverpool University.

In 1948 there came the first of many Middle East interludes scattered over my future, all connected in some way with blown sand. The top Shell management received an unusual request from a rival group to borrow my services for advice on the siting of a port for a new oil field about to be opened on the Qatar Peninsula in the Persian Gulf. Assurance was sought that the projected port would not be overwhelmed by sand dunes. I found the peninsula to be a bare, sandy flat, standing less than one metre above the sea. There was one ragged village of pearl divers and a great mound of stinking oyster shells. There were only a few coastal dunes, and they were unlikely to become a nuisance. Qatar was soon to become an industrial area ruled by a very wealthy sheikh.

The research staff at Thornton were happy and productive, and the technicians' unions were cooperative. I sensed, though, that my background was inadequate to cope with the great variety of industrial research projects in which the oilmen were involved, or to coordinate the host of different projects going on at three big centres of different nationalities. In 1949, with some reluctance, I resigned from Shell. Some years later, Lord Rothschild took on the job. I expect he did it much better.

Another reason for my leaving Shell was that at heart I am an explorer. I longed to get back to doing my own thing, to discovering more about the natural processes that have been going on for ages, unconcerned with man's needs and convenience. I wanted to find out the basic dynamic processes by which rivers transport sand, stones, and boulders along their beds, and what weight of solids a given stream can transport in a given time.

12

Rickwoods—Egyptian Fantasia— Algeria—Kuwait
1949–1952

I STILL RETAINED the London flat, but now we were a family of four, with Plankie, myself, Stephen, and Jane (who had arrived in 1948), plus a nurse. A larger house was needed, somewhere in the country and preferably accessible both to London and to Enid's family at Rottingdean. After a long and strenuous search (petrol was still rationed), I happened to find in Harrods's estate office particulars not yet circulated concerning a house called Rickwoods in the little parish of Mark Beech, near Edenbridge in West Kent. We went there at once. The sellers, Mr. and Mrs. Chatty, were in the midst of a big cocktail party but kindly managed to show us around. Plankie and I decided almost on the spot that at last we had found just the home we wanted.

Rickwoods is a large, roomy, late Victorian country house on a south-facing slope with a wide ten-mile view away to the ridge of Ashdown Forest. There is nothing but dairy farms around, yet it is within six minutes' walk of the Cowden railway station. It came with some nine acres of land. Electricity had just been installed. The structure of the house was solid and sound. The price was ridiculously low because some downstairs flooring needed replacement. I bought Rickwoods there and then, and it was our home for the next thirty-four years. Both children have always loved it. A few years ago age forced us to move to London, so we had to sell it—for thirty-five times what we paid.

For those who are able, there is great satisfaction in doing things oneself. It also saves a lot of money. I now had a large workshop-cum-study. The workshop was equipped with the tools necessary for most household trades, accumulated over three generations, starting with my grandfather's massive Indian teak workbench and carpenter's tools. I did all my own household carpentry, plumbing, wiring, surveying, drain laying, and tree felling. I also had acquired, long ago, a small precision lathe and the fine tools needed to make the delicate instruments I required for my laboratory work at Imperial College.

At Imperial College I started a series of "try-it-and-see" experiments examining how the presence of a dispersion of solid grains affects the flow of a liquid. The effect was known only for such low concentrations of solids that the influence of one grain on another could be neglected. Experiments demanded that the solids be kept dispersed, hence they had to be made the same density as the liquid. I made quantities of uniform spheres of the same density as water by the simple "shot-tower" method of allowing a stream of individual molten drops of a plastic mixture to fall through air from a thermostatically heated container, solidifying as they fell. As I increased the concentration of these grains in flowing water, the previously neglected effects of one grain on another became dominant. The liquid's resistance to shear rapidly increased, till finally the whole liquid-solid substance suddenly "froze" solid. Such experiments, spurned by engineers as impractical, threw a lot of light on what happens when a river carries a load of solids along its bed. In another experiment I put a high concentration of the same light grains into the shore end of a wave tank. The effect was remarkable: the whole of the wave energy was dissipated by intergranular friction.

I found that Perspex is an ideal laboratory material for experiments. With liquid chloroform as a solvent, it can be welded to build one-piece structures. Colourless and perfectly transparent, it is just the stuff to make an experimental water flume. I could watch every movement within a stream, including that of solids being transported along the bed. Working for long periods over open dishes of chloroform had no effect on me or others in the laboratory; it is not at all poisonous.

I had lost interest in the physics of blown sand and deserts because data were never available about long-term wind regimes—their strengths and directions—necessary for correlations with local sand movements and dune forms. Nevertheless, I found myself in some demand as a sage on the subject.

Early in 1951 I got an all-expenses-paid invitation (including Plankie) from the Egyptian government to join a gathering in Cairo, ostensibly to discuss desert problems and to celebrate the foundation of the Egyptian Desert Institute. In reality, it seemed to be an excuse for an international public relations exercise, paid for out of the money the late King Fuad had left to support the institute. It was a fantastic occasion. The five hundred or so guests included notables from many countries. From England had come the vice chancellors of both Oxford and Cambridge, the presidents of the Royal Colleges of Physicians and Surgeons, and others of like standing. A number of old friends had been invited, too: Pat Clayton (formerly a prisoner of war), several archaeologists, and Laslo Almasy, a Hungarian desert enthusiast we had known before the war who had lately served on Rommel's staff against us and had many interesting stories to tell. George Murray was there in his official capacity as director of the Egyptian Desert Survey. We all banqueted lavishly for a week, each night in a different palace.

Between events, Plankie and I joined forces with Bill Hance, an American professor from Columbia University. He and his wife had somehow acquired a car and driver, so we were able to see the sights independently. We have remained friends ever since. On the last evening we all dined at Abdin Palace with young King Farouk. Our long procession marched up the grand stairs. On each side, on every stair, stood a tall black Nubian, stiff as a statue and carrying a spear. We were ushered into the imposing throne room, introduced to the king by name, and shook hands. Farouk was a fat, wildly irresponsible young man, who nevertheless chatted easily and well and looked quite regal surrounded by his ministers in their splendid court uniforms.

We then passed into a still bigger hall. Against the whole of one wall were piled, ceiling high, an array of luscious dishes such as few of us had seen since before the war. Centre front rose a high dais on which stood a bowl of gold several feet in diameter. Behind it, a great grinning black Nubian in a red-and-gold gown ladled out drinks for us into gold goblets. I could easily picture him as (in former days) the court executioner Masrur in Flecker's *Hassan*. I saw the two vice chancellors standing together in awe. One said to the other, "I just don't believe it." Then we ate a buffet feast off solid-gold plates. We learned, sadly too late, that it would have been quite in order for guests to steal, as a souvenir, some small object such as a gold spoon.

That was probably the last time anyone would see traditional Oriental splendour.

In the spring of the same year, 1951, the French invited me to take part in a small but select desert symposium in Algeria. Another foreign member was Theodor von Kármán, one of the leading fluid-dynamicists of the time. He was then an old man, and he was attended by his elderly sister. A Hungarian, he spoke villainous French and even worse English. Notwithstanding, he was full of wisdom and fun. An aircraft took us from Algiers inland to the Grand Erg Occidental, a sand sea of large dunes of unusual form. It intrigued von Kármán to speculate on the particular type of wind regime responsible. We lived happily in tents. Later our aircraft took us to a military region. One day the French army threw a party for us. A whole ox had been roasting all day over a charcoal fire, spitted on a small, slowly turning tree trunk. That evening we sat on the open desert and were waited on by smartly dressed blacks, whom some might have regarded as slaves, each adorned with a pink rose in his hair. In Oriental style, we were invited to use our fingers to pick choice morsels of delicious, scorched flesh from the ox. The symposium ended in Algiers with a truly magnificent dinner.

Two other Middle East interludes followed in 1952. The new Israeli state had taken over from the British Palestine Mandate I had known, which had included the southern desert of the Negev between Sinai and Jordan. The Israelis were thereby stimulated to hold a symposium on desert physics of their own, in Jerusalem, and I was invited to take part. There was a good-sized gathering with people from several countries, including physicists, geologists, and a meteorologist or two from Australia. We were welcomed personally by David Ben Gurion, the great Jewish leader. He was a striking man with a big head of fluffed-out white hair. I lodged with the family of the scientist who organized the meeting, and I learned from my hostess about life in the kibbutz in which she had been brought up.

We were taken on tours, either south to the Negev or northward. I chose the latter as I already knew the Negev. We were driven along the Golan Heights, where we could look down over the cultivated Syrian plains below. The Moslem population had recently departed from the Israeli side, to remain permanently as refugees, battening on the world's generosity. They had been agriculturalists, and without them the orange and olive groves remained untended. Shoulder-high weeds stretched as far as one could see. Descending from the heights through quite mountainous country, we passed well-kept villages of a very different character from those we had seen elsewhere. A well-known American expert, oblivious of our Israeli guides, exclaimed loudly, "Gee, that's the first bit of decent farming I've seen in this God-damned country." They were not Israeli villages at all. They were the homes of Druze who had stayed rather than flee with the Moslems.

The Israelis were soon to overcome that agricultural disaster, but not without an initial setback. Rushing to help, Zionists in the United States had shipped over the latest in farm machinery, designed for the Great Plains. We saw the useless things parked in the corners of the little stony fields. However, within a short time these astonishing Jews had turned farmers, built their own machinery, and carried on.

A few months later I was asked by the Kuwait Oil Company to go out and report on the degree of possible danger to oil-field installations from encroaching sand, a problem that had troubled the American fields farther south. The leisured comfort, idleness, and anonymity of first-class air travel sometimes evokes strange confidences. On the flight from Cairo to Kuwait, I liked the look of my American neighbor. We began talking, and I asked what prompted him to fly out from the States with nothing but one carpetbag. He said he owned a fleet of supertankers, and one was stuck at Kuwait with a damaged rudder. "I like seeing to things myself," he said. "I'm going to see what the trouble is and sack the master for not giving me details. All my ships are self-sufficient when it comes to repairs, and I can fly in any part from one of my depots. It's that simple." After a while he added, "I've been in shipping all my life. I have no other interests. I've made a great deal of money. It's time I retired. But what shall I do? I have an oceangoing yacht, but I can't spend my life in it. I can't spend it swimming in my lake at home. I just don't know." He sat brooding—a very worried multimillionaire without a hobby to fall back on.

A hundred miles or so from Kuwait, I happened to look out the window. The whole evening sky ahead was red like a gorgeous sunset, but in the east instead of the west. Then I realized they were burning off the natural gas—at a rate greater than would keep all the gasworks of Europe supplied. What else could they do with it? There was no local industry; no liquification plants were then available, or special tankers to carry liquid gas. And this oil field was one of the most, if not the most, prolific in the world.

The company had built a town of their own some miles from the old town of Kuwait. My host was the chief engineer, an Anglo Persian oil man (later Anglo-Iranian, and finally BP). Oilmen do things on the grandest scale and are at the same time the most friendly and helpful people. We drove along the jetty by car—the longest jetty in the world, capable of berthing six supertankers of *Queen Elizabeth* size at the same time. He took me over to inspect his seawater distillation plant, again the biggest in the world (Kuwait had no natural supplies of drinking water).

The company was a joint offshoot of Gulf Oil of America and Anglo-Iranian. It was a novel experiment in manning. The Americans of Aramco, farther south along the Arabian coast, had had much difficulty with excessive turnover of their nationals due to homesickness, the long, oppressive summers, and their monotonous, barren surroundings. In the new company, Americans and British were deliberately mixed, from the field manager down. As a result, the British persuaded their American friends to join them in "huntin', shootin', and fishin'" expeditions during periods of local leave, and to take an interest in things outside their jobs. The turnover of Americans dropped dramatically.

All the company's buildings were thoroughly temperature controlled, with air-conditioning for the intense summer heat and heating for the icy winter winds from the Persian mountains across the gulf. I was interested to see how they dealt medically with heat problems experienced by the outdoor men—the surveyors and others—who had to work under the full sun at times when shade temperatures were over $50°C$ ($120°F$). They dealt with it firmly. Anyone down with so-called heatstroke was severely reprimanded by the field manager for carelessness in not taking enough salt tablets. (Little dishes of them stood on every table in the mess during each meal.) In the North African desert we had not taken salt tablets, and we never suffered from salt deficiency. We were always on a water ration, and so refrigerated more efficiently without excessive perspiration. Water shortage may, of course, restrict one's drinking.

Then one is liable to general dehydration, which happens to have much the same symptoms of lassitude and apathy attributed to heatstroke.

The foregoing interludes each lasted a few weeks at most. I hope that what I contributed in each case was thought worthwhile by my hosts who had paid all my fares and expenses. Meanwhile, Rickwoods and its land took up a lot of my time. For summer holidays we either took the children to the seaside, or Plankie and I went climbing in Switzerland with George Murray, formerly director of the Egyptian Desert Survey, and his wife Edith.

13

Physicists and Engineers—
A Basic Experiment
1953–1958

MY MAIN HOBBY continued to be an attempt to understand the physics underlying the mechanisms by which a stream of water transports solids along its bed at a definite rate. I felt sure that the physics must be basically the same as that for windblown sand, but operating in different conditions. Working in water makes observations and measurements much more difficult than in air, and more variables are involved. The wind blows over an open land surface, but a liquid stream must be contained between boundaries whose width and depth are relevant, as is the gravity slope. Furthermore, in studying the physics of windblown sand, I was able to reason freely, uninhibited by any traditional ideas. But a large and diffuse literature already existed on grain transport by streams—a multitude of speculative interpretations of conflicting results from uncoordinated experiments. No definite conclusions seemed to have emerged.

Studies of water flow need heavy equipment and were considered within the domain of engineers, not physicists. As a technologist, the engineer is dedicated to the service of man's material needs. He is employed to carry out particular projects in the most expedient way, projects designed for man's immediate benefit. Therefore his outlook is anthropocentric, though not, of course, in the extreme mediaeval sense. His opportunities for research into better ways of doing things are strictly limited by cost considerations to the immediate project at hand. His business employers are generally too shortsighted to spend money on research into the underlying natural processes, even though a better understanding of these would ultimately save a lot of money. Nor has the training of the hydraulic engineer been broad enough to embrace the discipline of the physicist's reasoning.

In contrast, the physicist turns his back on man's needs and tries instead to understand processes of nature that operate oblivious of man, as they have done since the beginning, ages before man evolved, in blind obedience to apparently universal laws. The physicist is therefore suspicious of assumptions that savour in any way of man's wishfulness. Many widely held traditions have been found to be wrong simply because someone spotted a false assumption previously taken as axiomatic.

There is, in consequence, a wide difference in ideology between the engineer and the physicist. The older the technology, generally the wider the gap, as the original broad general reasoning becomes progressively replaced in engineering textbooks by contracted versions limited to narrower practical applications. A physicist without a mental reorientation would in general make a bad engineer, and vice-versa.

The engineer's working knowledge of water flow rests largely on physical principles evolved in the eighteenth century. As any given fluid can reasonably be assumed to be of the same density everywhere, those wise men realized that fluid motion could be generalized and simplified by eliminating the constant density, and thus converting the real dynamics into a kinematic representation. Thus, a fluid stress became a velocity squared, and fluid energy was represented by gravity height. This kinematic way of thinking was so useful, and had become so general, that by the start of the twentieth century it had become confused with reality.

The movement of solids along the beds of rivers and canals had become an important economic nuisance. The rates of grain movement needed to be predicted. Quite naturally it was assumed, tacitly and as a reasonable approximation, that although the solids were heavier than water, the difference in density could be ignored, thus allowing the kinematic way of thinking to remain applicable. This assumption being strictly tacit, and probably often unconscious, it was some time before I realized its existence and implications. It followed inescapably that all theories based on this assumption that purport to predict the separate movement of solids by water flow must be self-defeating. Furthermore, according to kinematic thinking, granular solids must glide frictionlessly over a streambed without dissipating energy—this in spite of the everyday evidence of the loud rattling of pebbles along the bed of a brook. This strangely unrealistic way of thinking persisted in one form or another for half a century. It still has some adherents.

It became clear to me that I would have to start afresh, returning to the reality of dynamics. As I saw it, I had to deal primarily with the shearing of a previously unstudied substance consisting of a dispersion of granular solids within a liquid. As a snooker player, I knew that when the cue ball strikes another ball a glancing blow, both balls move away from one another with momentum components at right angles to the original direction of the cue ball. So I expected that the random collisions that must occur when a dispersion of solids is sheared would amount to a dispersive pressure. This pressure would be exerted on a boundary which would resist further dispersion.

The simplest, and indeed only, practical way to confirm this would be to shear dispersions of my neutral-density grains in the annular space between two concentric drums, the outer of which was rotated. The dispersive pressure could be measured as a static pressure inside the inner drum wall, which would be made from deformable material. The shear stress could be measured at the same time by the torque on the inner drum. I rigged up the apparatus at home in my workshop and used my lathe to drive the outer drum at a wide range of speeds.

The most important result of this rotating drum experiment was that, independent of both solids' concentration and shear rate, the resistance attributable to the solids was always on the order of half the dispersive pressure. That is, the coefficient of solid to solid friction for a sheared dispersion of granular solids is virtually the same as that for the same solids in continuous contact. The fluid shear stress needed to push a known immersed weight of solids along the bed of a stream was now known. The immersed weight of solids in transit over a bed of the same solids cannot be measured, because one cannot isolate the moving from the stationary grains. But the rate of mass transport of an immersed weight of solids is easily measured, in the laboratory at least. And the fluid shear stress times the velocity of its action is the rate at which the fluid does transporting work. So I now saw clearly that the transport rate of solids must depend primarily on a rate of fluid energy supply, or in other words, on stream power. The transport rate did not, as had been previously thought, depend alone on either stream velocity or bed shear stress, but on the product of both. This, I felt, began to put the subject of the transport of solids by water on a sound footing.

14

Luna Leopold—Washington, D.C.
1956–1964

SOMETIME IN 1956 I was approached by Luna B. Leopold, then head of the Water Resources Division of the United States Geological Survey, with the idea of possible collaboration. We took to one another from the start. Officially his job entailed maintaining a detailed knowledge of all the natural water supplies in the country, both in quantity and quality. This meant establishing and running gauging stations on the rivers to record the day-to-day variations in the discharge, as well as the collection of other data. In reality, Luna Leopold's interests were much wider. A naturalist himself, and the son of the well-known naturalist Aldo Leopold, his interests lay largely in geomorphology, a field which considers how the earth's surface has been moulded by natural processes, and in particular the action of rivers in carrying away the debris of weathering and depositing it elsewhere. It is also of direct national importance because the processes have a bearing on the ever-decreasing water supply. Five southwestern states—California, Utah, Nevada, Arizona, and New Mexico—rely primarily on the Colorado River for their water. The annual floodwater is stored behind a succession of dams and used during the dry season. But as the rivers transport solids, the storage basins become progressively filled with sediments. Hence the need, in the long term, to be able to predict the annual rate at which rivers transport solids.

Leopold was impressed, as I was, with the absence of a basic understanding of the subject and with the apparent lack of desire to find out more. Here was a man of strong character and great practical experience, a nationwide authority in his field, and with the backing of a far-sighted director. We agreed that we ought to "stir the pool of complacent tradition with the stick of reality." He suggested that with his practical help and influence, I should try to find the stick—an explanation of how the laws of nature operate to make rivers behave as they do in moulding their channels according to their individual flow conditions. All of the U.S. river records would be available to me.

In 1958 I was duly taken on as a consultant to the U.S. government on the understanding that I spend a month each year in the States. In order to receive my salary I had to be sworn in as a federal employee. The list of undertakings involved in this swearing-in was what one might expect, reasonable and commonsense; but the pledge not to make war on the United States had been crossed out. Seemingly, it would be wrong for a government to ask anyone other than one of its own nationals to refrain from making war on it. A nice thought.

Washington, D.C., or properly, the District of Columbia, is a little semiautonomous enclave carved out of Virginia and Maryland to serve as the independent seat of the federal government. Apart from its well-planned layout and lack of both tall buildings and antiquity, Washington has a surprisingly English appearance. Luna managed to get me a room at the Cosmos Club, within easy walking distance of the U.S. Geological Survey office building. Life in a government office in Washington raised a faraway memory of my months in Whitehall in 1919, while I was waiting to go up to Cambridge. I think what impressed me most was the great rationality. Instead of having to spend half one's lunch hour walking to some restaurant and back again, here one merely stepped down to the cafeteria floor of the same building, where a remarkably good meal could be had at a remarkably low price and eaten in uncrowded comfort. The State Department cafeteria, for instance, is a single vast room, occupying the whole floor, that can lunch two thousand inmates without crowding or delay. Outside, too, one finds rationality in unexpected places. The basement of a new church is a car park instead of a musty crypt, a convenience to worshippers without any definable sacrilege.

On my trip to the West a decade earlier, my hotel room in San Francisco overlooked a big lighted sign, "The Experienced Traveler goes by Train." It was true then. Rail travel was at its zenith. I rode from San Francisco to Los Angeles in the most prestigious train of all, the Lark. It was a continuous, jointed tube—one long, well-furnished drawing room. On a straight section of track, I could look right down the center of the train, through the end observation car, to see the retreating countryside. The service was perfect.

Ten years later, having to go from Washington to Boston to give a talk at the Massachusetts Institute of Technology, I chose to go by train so as to see more of the country. Tradition said that the Bostonian was a luxury train. It happened that we ran into bad weather, with heavy, cold snow. The train stopped. The electric locomotive detached itself and disappeared ahead, presumably to reconnoitre, leaving the train without heat. It was away for an hour. This happened repeatedly. We found the buffet car locked and abandoned. All the water in the train froze. I joined a Boston lawyer and we shared what food we had. Luckily, he had a flask of whisky. No train staff bothered to appear. The train might have contained cattle. We finally reached Boston long after midnight, seven hours late. A noisy crowd of some hundred was milling round the information desk. I was to be met by Professor John Miller, a close friend of Luna Leopold. My lawyer friend kindly offered me a bed, but I explained doubtfully that I was to be met by a friend of a friend, someone I had never met. "Right," he said. "Let's see if we can spot a Harvard professor type among this lot." He dived into the crowd and by some magic produced John Miller within a minute. I am really grateful to that sharp-eyed lawyer.

The golden age of long-distance rail travel was clearly gone in America. Passenger traffic was losing money and was actively discouraged. I was sorry, for I used to enjoy a long train journey. As a boy, I had experienced the excitement of the night journey through France to the Alps, wakened at dawn by the clatter of milk cans and getting cups of delicious coffee handed through the train window. Later, in 1921, had come the fascination of the three-day journey in the Orient Express to Constantinople. Much as on a long sea voyage, one regarded newcomers as intruders to one's coziness and looked out aloofly as a local war was stopped to let this train from another world pass through. Then there were those nostalgic Indian occasions when, as I was breakfasting sleepily at some wayside station, the guard would murmur diffidently, "The train should be on its way if the sahib has quite finished." There were those slow day-long journeys through China, with so many strange things to see. The rhythmic jog-jog, jog-jog of wheels on rail joints was a more soothing background indication of speed than the monotonous humming of an aircraft going ten times as fast.

The morning after my long train journey to Boston, I saw the main street lined on each side with a chain of seven-foot-long snow mounds, which reduced the sidewalks to narrow trenches. A stalwart with a snow shovel was laboriously excavating his car from its mound when a powerful road clearer roared past. The poor fellow's car was reburied even deeper than before. The inhabitants of Boston were unconcerned, being used to that way of winter life.

On one occasion during those earlier years I had been asked to join a conference convened by a large mining company in Nevada to deal with the problem of preventing acres of arsenic-laden wastes from being blown by the wind and poisoning the surrounding countryside. I stayed in Las Vegas. As a national pleasure centre, to quote the Khalif in Flecker's *Hassan*, that city "hath a monstrous quality like the hind quarters of an elephant." Its airport concourse was so packed with slot machines that they were spewing out onto the tarmac. I had booked at the Stardust, one of a number of hotels on the two-thousand-bedroom scale found along the glittering Golden Mile. My taxi took me to a side entrance. Exploring, I found that the grand front entrance led directly into a vast foyer in almost complete darkness. It was filled with row upon row of fruit machines, whose tiny single lights gave the only illumination. I counted seven hundred of these things, standing like a regiment of soldiers on parade. Here and there, a few zombies pulled handles haphazardly, hoping no doubt to get something without paying. A bored guard with a revolver wandered round. I have never understood why these things abound in such numbers; I rarely saw anyone patronizing them. Perhaps they are a status symbol. Passages led away from the foyer to numerous gambling saloons, banqueting halls, conference rooms, and so on.

In contrast to the general garish exuberance my room was simple, yet it provided everything I wanted, at a surprisingly modest cost. I found a quiet region of the hotel for serious residents, with a good restaurant having attentive service. Las Vegas certainly caters well to all tastes.

In 1960 the family flew out to Washington with me. After staying a day or two with Luna and Carolyn Leopold, we flew on to Denver, Colorado, where we met Luna's unmarried sister Estella, a leading paleobotanist. I have a vivid memory of an evening when brother and sister, each with a guitar, sang Spanish songs together. On their mother's side, the Leopolds were descended from an old Spanish family who had settled in New Mexico in the seventeenth century. The wife of a Geological Survey friend of Luna's, whom we remember only as BJ, took us to a ski resort high up in the Rockies. Stephen and Jane, then aged fourteen and twelve, had their first experiences of falling into deep snowdrifts. After that, we were taken on a private tour arranged by Luna. We went first to the Grand Canyon of the Colorado River. We had the energy to tramp from the little hotel at the rim of the canyon down the zigzag mule track to the bottom, a mile down in altitude. Rather than risk muleback on such a track, we decided to walk. This journey took us through rock strata spanning half the history of the earth. Near the river the vegetation became almost tropical. We then traveled on to the Painted Desert of Arizona, and back via the Glen Canyon Dam, then under construction.

Plankie and the children were to fly home to England from New York City. This gave us the opportunity to stay with our old friends Bill and Margery Hance, whom we had met during the Egyptian fantasia nine years before. I rejoined Luna in Washington.

Over the years we have enjoyed a number of visits by the Leopolds to Rickwoods. In 1963 it was arranged that Madelyn Leopold, who was about Jane's age, would spend a month with us there. One of the lures was the ponies. Jane had her Pixie, and we hired another pony for Madelyn, to whom riding was a novelty. Madelyn came over by sea in what must have been one of the last great transatlantic mail liners. I went to meet her at Southampton and found a quiet, outwardly self-possessed young lady of fifteen waiting alone on the quayside. That five-day journey by herself must have needed a lot of courage, for her and for her parents. The following year Jane flew to the United States, by herself, to spend a month with the Leopolds at their house on the outskirts of Washington.

I spent much time visiting hydraulic laboratories in various parts of the United States, but I could find no work going on other than ad hoc experiments in aid of particular commercial projects. I could find no institutions interested in studying sediment transport as a process of nature, or even in trying to discover the reason why existing experimental results remained grossly inconsistent. Discussions with Luna led to his decision that the U.S. Geological Survey would have to embark on its own experiments, designed on scientific rather than engineering lines. I outlined the series of experiments I had in mind.

Soon thereafter, Luna Leopold and his assistant, William Emmett, built a hydraulics laboratory. Though it was housed in an old factory, it was modern and efficient. Luna assigned a young colleague, Garnet Williams, to carry out our experiments. The idea was to change only one factor at a time. The results paid off. They showed conclusively that a stream of water of a given power can transport solids along its bed at a progressively decreasing rate as the flow depth is increased. In other words, the transport rate is an inherent function of the flow depth, a fact that had not previously occurred to anyone. I found that when the transport rates measured by other workers in earlier flume experiments were corrected to the rates corresponding to a constant, standard flow depth, the supposedly gross inconsistencies disappeared. The earlier measurements had been wrongly interpreted.

15

With Leopold in Wyoming
1967–1974

THE TRANSPORT RATE of solids is easily measured in a laboratory flume by collecting and weighing them as they fall out of the downstream end. But a river has no end, so reliable measurements in rivers had long remained an unsolved problem. Samples of the material moving along the bed had been trapped using a heavily weighted collector like a squat, open-mouthed toad with its lower lip flush with the natural bed surface and a net body which allowed the water current to pass through. A set of samples could be taken across a river's width, but there was no method of testing the reliability of such a sampling method. So what use were the years of laboratory experiments as long as we could not compare the results with the reality of actual rivers?

I insisted, and Luna readily agreed, that another once-and-for-all experiment was essential, even though an expensive engineering project would be involved. A suitable river must be temporarily diverted to allow construction of a concrete channel across and beneath its bed. The channel would be provided with a gate built flush with the natural bed surface. A conveyor belt inside the channel would carry all the solids that fell in through the opened gates to the bank for weighing. A light footbridge across the river would allow us at the same time to lower a sampler to the bed and raise it after a known time at a succession of sites. The transport rates as computed from the sampler weights could thus be compared with the directly measured rate. We would then know for the first time the reliability of the practical sampler method of measurement. The detailed design of the apparatus would be tricky because once the river was restored to its course, it would never be possible to do any repairs or adjustments to the remote-controlled hydraulic mechanisms operating the vital gates.

In his favorite part of the highland state of Wyoming Luna had built, with his own hands, a comfortable three-room log cabin to be his summer resort. He had chosen a site within easy reach of several rivers whose behaviour had a special interest due to their large seasonal ranges of discharges resulting from spring snowmelt in the mountains. He already had one of these rivers, the East Fork, in mind for the project, its upper reaches being free of beaver dams.

I was introduced into an entirely new world, a world of great distances and sparse population. Wyoming is a land of wild, snowy mountains, beaver-wrecked streams, large cattle ranches, and cowboys on horseback wearing traditional broad-brimmed Stetson hats (I had to wear one to conform with local custom).

From the small airport at Rock Springs we drove for three hours across barren sagebrush country around six thousand feet above sea level, passing no human habitation and only very occasionally another vehicle on the road. Nearing the mountains, the sagebrush gave way to lush grasslands watered by streams fed mainly by snowmelt. Finally we came to a roadside notice,

PINEDALE

POP 951

It was a three-hour drive northward through the mountains before another human habitation came into sight. Our truck climbed more and more steeply up the mountainside, past a glacier-scooped lake, and up until it could go no farther. We walked the short way to

Luna's cabin, which had remained locked since the previous fall. From the balcony I looked out westward, over the lake below surrounded by silver birches, and below that the little township, and away beyond over rolling grassland to another distant range of snow-capped mountains. It was a truly lovely site for a summer cabin.

It seems that the organisms that cause wood rot cannot survive in regions where the winters are extremely cold. Wood structures in the higher Alps, for instance, rarely rot. In building his cabin, and later his log house, Luna had collected old logs left lying about from former times. Many were a century old, yet perfectly sound.

The main feature inside was the big stone hearth for an open log fire. Hinged brackets projected from the walls on which cook pots could be hung and swung to any desired position. Luna could do anything with that fireplace. He could bring a smouldering log to life with one deft kick; he could fry eggs and bacon, roast a joint, or bake bread in a heavily lidded iron pot buried under an accumulation of hot ashes.

The first morning there, I walked down to our truck to fetch a screwdriver. I surprised a bear inside it.

I found Pinedale to be a genuine working centre, catering mainly to the area's cattle ranches. It lacked a hotel and there were no tourists. There was a gas station selling cylinders of propane, and a hardware store and supermarket, both of which might be envied by a fair-sized city. A small, friendly bar was popular with the locals, and there was an eating house. The isolated community was entirely self-sufficient. It had to be, for from October to April it would be under three feet of snow at a temperature of $-30°C$ [$-20°F$].

The mountain snow was melting and the river was rising fast, overflowing some of the surrounding land. We found a stretch of bank high enough to remain dry, and Luna made a detailed survey of the site with a boat we had brought. On a succeeding visit to Wyoming I found that Luna and his engineers had built our concrete channel on the river site. They had done a wonderful job. The whole installation was not only complete but had survived lying frozen hard all winter. The gates, submerged on the riverbed, could be opened and closed at the touch of a button. The wide conveyor belt carried sand and gravel to the bank where it was raised by a bucket lift and tipped into the hopper of a big weighing machine, whence another belt carried it away, back into the river downstream. Luna's colleague, Bill Emmett, took charge of the sampling, experimenting to find the most reliable and systematic ways of doing things. He later analyzed his samples for the size distributions of the grains. We thus had a complete record of everything that was going down the river. It was soon clear that a computation of the entire transport rate made from the samples, if carefully taken, agreed well with the direct-check measurements. This meant that the transport rates of solids by natural rivers could, for the first time, be measured with reasonable confidence.

Using the mass of data obtained from the East Fork installation I could correlate the changes in the transport rates with corresponding changes in the river's discharge. I concluded that natural, unconstrained river channels in loose, erodable material must in some degree be inherently unstable. The eighteenth-century savant Daniel Bernoulli had ignored the random energy of internal turbulence when formulating his theorem on stream energy. Since students in river engineering were taught that this, like other eighteenth-century theorems, expressed gospel truth, the effects of variations in the turbulent energy along a river channel had been overlooked. Any flow divergence due to a local increase in width or depth is accompanied by an increase in turbulent energy, with a resulting increase in boundary erosion. This further augments the local cause, and so on. The eroded material is deposited downstream, thus causing a reversal of the process. Depending on the material, the basic instability may take several forms—a rhythmic succession of deeps and shallows, or a meander, or both together.

The same natural process explains another mystery: why, at the same river discharge, the measured transport of solids may be considerably greater while the river is rising than when it is falling. During a rise, the deeps are being scoured deeper, with consequently greater material transport, while during a fall the deeps trap material so that less is measured.

On the whole, I believe that Luna Leopold and I contributed a good deal of new knowledge to the world. We had found a sound stick and were beginning to stir the pool.

About this time, interest in the transport of solids by rivers was developing in several parts of the world. Data were becoming available from various rivers of different sizes and characteristics. It occurred to me to apply the corrections for flow depth and grain size revealed by Garnet Williams's laboratory experiments to natural rivers, although the conditions seemed very different. As I half expected, the same corrections brought the river data into line. I was astonished at the apparent worldwide consistency, from tiny laboratory streams only a few centimeters deep to the mighty Zaire River six miles wide and seventy feet deep, and from the transport of fine sand to the movement of boulders by flash floods.

During my visit in 1966 Luna organized a diversion. We were to traverse, on rafts, the whole hundred and more miles of the Colorado River through Cataract Canyon, which leads down into the Grand Canyon. We were doing this, ostensibly, to measure the depths of the great pools between successive cataracts. This stretch of river had been rafted before, but rarely, and only when the river was in full flood. We were a party of eight: Luna, Bill Emmett, me, two experienced boatmen, and three other colleagues of Luna's whose names I have forgotten. We embarked on the Green River in Utah, the main tributary of the Colorado, a big, placid stream which we cruised down for some miles. We had two rafts, each consisting of an army pontoon surmounted by a stout timber frame carrying one powerful outboard motor, the sole means of steering. The expedition was well thought out. We each had a big waterproof bag for our bedding and belongings and a life jacket. All the gear was thoroughly lashed down.

The grassy banks gradually gave way to vertical rock walls as we entered Labyrinth Canyon. Then came the deep-canyon junction with the Colorado, flowing past from left to right, swollen with snowmelt from the Rockies. High on the rock wall was painted, in large letters, "ALL CRAFT TURN LEFT" and a great arrow that pointed upstream. On the right, grim warnings forbade going downstream, further emphasized by a very large skull and crossbones. In addition, an ominous dull roar rose up from the water and echoed between the canyon walls. We ignored the warnings and turned downstream.

Some way ahead the broad ribbon of water abruptly ended. Nothing could be seen beyond. We were being carried inevitably toward a brink. There was little time to speculate about what lay beyond. The rafts were suddenly thrown about like corks by a chaos of raging water. We lay flat on the deck, clinging tightly to stout timber baulks. I had a quick vision of skimming round the rim of a huge whirlpool and started to wonder whether, if we slipped down into it, we could ever climb out. Then, a moment later, we were rushing headlong into a high-standing wall of water. The raft rose like a horse taking a fence. We had met a giant hydraulic jump. The next moment the raft heeled over to such an angle that I expected it to capsize. The descent of that cataract seemed endless, but it probably took but a few long minutes. This first of the cataracts would have brought certain death to anyone in a light pleasure craft. Suddenly we were cruising calmly over the smooth water of a deep pool several miles long. Then came another roaring cataract, even more hair-raising.

The vertical rock walls towered upward on either side of us. But now and then we passed isolated bits of beach where a rockfall had piled debris above the water level. We landed on one of the beaches for a meal, and later found another suitable for a night's camp. In one region where the land surface above was lower, a meander loop had doubled back on itself. Climbing a rock ridge, we looked down on the strange sight of two great rivers flowing side by side in opposite directions less than fifty yards apart.

Luna's organization of that trip extended to arranging for his friend Herb Skibisky to fly his helicopter down to our camp at the bottom of the canyon in case we might need more supplies.

The whole journey took several days, shooting down cataract after cataract. It ended on a new lake-reservoir created by the Glen Canyon Dam we had seen being built some years before. I thoroughly enjoyed that trip, the recurring thrill of each cataract, the camping and sleeping in the open on little rocky beaches under the stars. It brought back so many memories of old times. There was the evening chatter over the day's adventures (none of us had had any like experience before). There was exultation at our survival, coupled with admiration for the boatmen's skill, and a background sense of awe at the overwhelming blind destructive power of uncontrolled nature.

I am sure I cannot have thought of it at the time, but on writing this, I realize that I was then over seventy.

The last time I stayed with Luna in Pinedale was in 1974. There had been a divorce, and both he and Carolyn had remarried. In 1974 Luna had almost finished building a large new log house on a bit of land provided by a friendly ranch owner. Plankie came with me on this visit. She flew directly to San Francisco to stay a week with Barbara (the new Mrs. Leopold) at their winter house in Berkeley across the bay. Meanwhile, Luna and I put the finishing touches on the Pinedale house, making everything ready for Plankie's arrival. It was sparkling spring weather in early June, though at that altitude there was a morning frost on the trout stream flowing under the veranda and a cold wind blew. Luna had retired early from the U.S. Geological Survey and was now professor of geology at the University of California in Berkeley. He had some students with him in Pinedale. When Plankie arrived, she found herself playing hostess with only the open log hearth for cooking. It was fun learning. We spent odd moments stuffing moss into the chinks between the wall logs to keep out the icy draughts.

We have continued to be close friends with both Carolyn and Bill Michaels, and Barbara and Luna Leopold. The Leopolds flew over from California for my ninetieth birthday, a thoughtful gesture and one very much appreciated. The Michaelses visited us the same year.

16

Meanwhile and Elsewhere
1966–1974

IN 1966 I flew to Iraq at the request of a firm of consulting engineers to advise them on a new and unexpected dune problem. The area of ancient Mesopotamia consists of great plains of dried, silty mud deposited over the ages from inundations by the Tigris and Euphrates rivers. There had never been a sand dune problem in modern times. A new canal was being dug, as canals had been dug for millennia. But now an advancing chain of small dunes threatened to choke the canal. What was causing them? What to do about it?

As I had guessed, the cause was gross overgrazing. Left to itself, the desert surface of Iraq acquires a thin protective crust from seasonal dew. As we were cruising around to look at the very sparse vegetation, we saw a clear demonstration of the dust-raising mechanism. Stopping to eat our sandwiches under a cloudless, clear blue sky, we noticed a little isolated dust cloud drifting by. Looking back, I saw that it was coming from our own tracks, and from nowhere else. Our wheels, disturbing the surface, had left tiny sharp-edged ridges which the breeze could tear away and disintegrate. Looking around, we found that at each small vegetation patch the ground was pocked with thousands of small hoof marks. Market conditions had become such that the villagers along the rivers found it easier to raise flocks of sheep and goats than to cultivate their land, even though the government had dug irrigation trenches for them.

Nothing immediate could be done about that, so I turned to examining the extent of the local menace. Enquiries indicated that the dune movement was sufficiently slow that sand which got into the canal could be periodically cleared, just as it had been done in past ages. "That would not be possible," I was told. "The Iraqi government does not provide any money for maintenance." Plenty of money was available for capital projects and for armaments, but nothing for looking after what had been already paid for—just like improvident children with too much pocket money.

Alongside one silted-up canal we came on a huge "walking dragline" lying abandoned. The thing was as big as a house. It could walk along a canal line on great stumpy, flat-footed legs. A long boom could reach out across a canal, and from a pulley on its end a shovel could be dragged home, scooping out successive cuts. The shovel was lying on the ground. We drove our Land Rover into it, with several feet to spare on either side. Each scoop of that shovel could remove many tons of mud.

In the early spring of 1968 I was asked, through an agent, to advise the Arab government of Abu Dhabi on the best place for a new motor road to Buraimi Oasis which would have to cross a continuous wall of shifting sand dunes. Oil had recently been discovered there and production had already started. I would be seeing things from the host's side rather than the oilmen's.

The region has an odd history. The mouth of the Persian Gulf is closed, save for the narrow Strait of Hormuz, by a horn of desert that juts out eastward from Arabia. Five small independent sheikhdoms have long occupied the inward, gulf side of this horn. Abu Dhabi is the largest, lying next door to what is now Saudi Arabia. On maps of the last century the region was shown as the Pirate Coast. The land was so poor and waterless that piracy must have been one of the few possible ways of life. Piracy became such a

menace to trade that the British Indian government finally arranged
a truce with the local sheikhs. It is intriguing to speculate on the
terms of that understanding. That it remained but a truce suggests
that the terms were diplomatically doubtful. I like to think a shrewd
British agent suggested with flowery vagueness that smuggling
might not only be more profitable, but also safer and far more re-
spectable than piracy. Moreover, the British might then turn a blind
eye. Anyhow, the pirates became smugglers in a big way, without
hindrance from the British, and everyone was happy. Before the oil
age burst upon it, the tiny sheikhdom of Dubai was, after the United
States, the largest importer of Swiss watches in the world. On
newer maps, the Pirate Coast has been changed to the United Arab
Emirates.

I found Abu Dhabi in the midst of a transformation from an in-
significant little sheikhdom to an important oil state. A score of
cargo ships had lain in wait for weeks to unload at a congested
quayside. Hired Pakistani workers swarmed around. A row of small
modern villas had been built along the shore, each with a bit of
walled garden, filled, for lack of water, with dry sand. Sheikh Zaid,
installed only a couple of years previously, had suddenly found
himself an absolute ruler with two million pounds a week pocket
money. He was taking things calmly in stride, sorting out the sharks
from the dolphins among the host of clamouring contractors. These
sheikhly families produce men with a seemingly inborn capacity for
doing the right thing.

At Buraimi Oasis, a hundred miles inland across the desert, I was
astonished to find, all by himself, my old friend Hugh Boustead (I
learned later that he was Sir Hugh, KBE, CMG, DSO, MC). An energetic
individualist about my age, he had been a midshipman early in the
First World War. He deserted (a heinous crime) because he feared
that he would miss the fighting. He then enlisted in the infantry
under another name and quickly earned a commission. He did so
well that when discovered, his crime was most exceptionally overlooked. Having recovered from serious war wounds, he joined the
British military mission with Denikin's ill-fated White Russian

army during the Bolshevik Revolution. After that, he became a member of the British army boxing team. An all-round athlete, he qualified for the Olympic Games. Later, as an officer in the Sudan Defense Force, Hugh spent his periods of leave on various expeditions. He climbed in the Himalayas, joined my 1932 Sudan expedition, and the following year was a member of Hugh Routledge's Mount Everest expedition.

During the Second World War Boustead fought in the Ethiopian campaign. Since he spoke fluent Arabic and had a great liking for the people, he spent the rest of the war as political agent in various parts of Arabia, and finally in Abu Dhabi. The then sheikh, a difficult man with a mind in a past century, refused to spend a single rupee on any development for his tribe's good. Losing patience, Boustead, with the tribe's consent, engineered his replacement by his younger brother Zaid, a man of great ability and charm. Boustead then retired to live out his life in peace, in the shadow of his friend Zaid. He had the honourific title of Master of the Ruler's Horse. He died some years later, having written a very interesting autobiography, *The Wind of Morning*. Zaid is now the very respected president of the United Arab Emirates.

The next year, 1969, I was invited to America to receive the Warren Prize awarded by the National Academy of Sciences. Since the United States is so big, some U.S. learned societies hold their meetings in turn in different states rather than centrally in Washington. This meeting took place in New Hampshire. It was during the fall, so the maple trees covering the hills were in full colour. I remember a very pleasant informal dinner. Luna Leopold was there as an academician. Unique in the academy's history, three siblings of the one family were members—Luna, his brother, and his sister Estella had been elected independently on their own merits.

During my visit I was taken to see the army's nearby cold research station. A smart young GI collected me from my hotel. We talked during the drive, and I happened to ask how long he was likely to stay in his present job. He answered quite simply, "I'm posted to the South Pole next week." Among the items of interest I saw was an enlarged photo of a railway track mistakenly laid over permafrost. The track had been so distorted that it undulated between steep hills and deep valleys. I was shown round the cold rooms where they stored six-foot-long cores cut from the Antarctic ice, kept at their original temperatures for scientific study. Each room was labeled according to its temperature: $-30°C$, $-40°C$, and so on. Swathed in plastic, the cores stood in rows like huge white cigars. It was interesting to note that although my guide and I were in shirtsleeves, due to the still air I didn't begin to feel the intense cold for fully five minutes.

I returned once again to America in 1970, this time at the invitation of the Geological Society of America. I was to receive the Penrose Gold Medal, their highest award for "eminent research in pure geology." This was a bit strange, as I was not and never had been a professional geologist. Plankie was included in the invitation, which was very kind and thoughtful. There were over two thousand geologists from the United States and Canada at the presentation, which took place in Milwaukee, Wisconsin, during the society's annual get-together. There was a fulsome citation, and I had to make a suitable acceptance speech. There was also a huge dinner. During the week we were able to see something of the city. The inhabitants are largely of German origin, and the principal industry is beer making. Appropriately, each member of the gathering was given a large beer mug as a souvenir.

A little later that year the Geological Society of London awarded me their Wollaston Medal. The medal is made of palladium, an uncommon element that had been discovered by the geologist Wollaston. It is a brilliant white metal of the platinum group. It was pleasing that my work was thus recognized on both sides of the Atlantic, particularly since it was not in geology proper but in the natural processes underlying it.

In the summer of 1970 I flew to Teheran at the request of the international oil consortium (formerly the Anglo-Persian Oil Company) to advise them on the likelihood of sand encroaching on the field installations near the head of the Persian Gulf. Talking with the top executives, I found it rather hard to distinguish Persians from Englishmen or Americans. They all spoke the same brand of English and called each other by their forenames or nicknames. I flew in one of the consortium's aircraft over the Bakhtiari Mountains to Ahwaz, which is located near the mouth of the Shatt-el-Arab waterway. It was the hottest time of the year at Ahwaz, but every room and car was well refrigerated. I had a helicopter to take me round the oil fields. There were, indeed, some small sand accumulations, but nothing that could not be easily dealt with once I had found the mean annual direction from which the sand was drifting. This may not coincide with the conventional annual direction, and needs computing from five or ten years of original daily records, only available at some nearby meteorological station.

The nearest established meteorological station was sixty miles away, near the great refinery complex of Abadan. There I found an intelligent young man in charge who spoke good English. In the course of my two days' work of analyzing the wind records, I had several talks with him which left me increasingly puzzled as to his origin. Eventually I asked outright whether he was Persian. He answered proudly, "I am a Bakhtiari. The governments come and go, but we have always lived in those mountains. The Persian army leaves us alone. They've never conquered us." He chuckled, "You should see my father's house. It simply bristles with guns we've taken from them." Still puzzled, I asked, "Are you Moslem?" He said, "Yes, for convenience. Traditionally we are fire worshippers." I asked what that meant. He said, "It's like this. If you and I were camping together and you started to put out the fire, I should be very angry, thinking you were trying to kill my God." Boldly I asked, "How far do you believe it?" He answered, "How much of your religion do you believe?" We changed the subject with a smile.

That talk with the educated son of an ancient, fiercely independent mountain tribe stuck in my mind. The Truth to any one person is what that particular person has been led to believe, partly by tradition and partly by experience. Hence, as that very shrewd administrator Pontius Pilate well knew, Truth differs from person to person, and so is undefinable. When the same information from two sources happens to be contradictory, the human brain is unconsciously capable of believing both versions. Like the Red Queen in Lewis Carroll's *Alice's Adventures In Wonderland,* the brain seems able "to believe half a dozen impossible things before breakfast." This "red queen ability" seems very evident in religion, politics, and everyday life.

As I was driven back to Ahwaz, the temperature was around 50°C (120°F). A car air-conditioner takes nearly half the engine's power, and when the radiator began to leak, the driver thought it best to turn the cooling off. With the sun burning on the car roof, the heat inside became almost unbearable. We were losing so much water that the engine began to falter. By stopping to fill up at every irrigation ditch that wasn't dry, we just managed to crawl home to Ahwaz. I think that was the hottest journey I ever made.

17

Later
1974–1986

WITH INCREASING AGE and inactivity life's memorable events occur less often. Lengthening periods of routine slip by unnoticed. The false impression results that time is speeding up. I was doing a fair amount of writing during these years.

One memorable event in 1977 occurred when I was asked by the National Aeronautics and Space Administration (NASA) to give the keynote address at a meeting of geologists and other space scientists. The meeting was to compare the desert landscapes of Earth and Mars. It was held for a week at Palm Desert, a new, up-and-coming offshoot of Palm Springs in Southern California. The site of the meeting had been specially chosen for the desert character of its surroundings. However, during that week it rained every day. The main thoroughfare through the town, labeled Bob Hope Street, was still only dirt. It was all but washed away.

NASA had recently sent spacecraft to orbit Mars and had succeeded in landing an unmanned craft to take close-up pictures. Those photos of the landscape revealed apparent sand dune forms much like those here on Earth, in spite of the vastly different atmosphere. This had already started theories, but it was, and still is, mere guesswork as to what the stuff of the so-called dunes really is. We have no tangible evidence, and won't have until some of it is brought back to Earth. Is it granular like sand, or fluffy like snowflakes? And we still have but little idea of the scale of the dune heights.

We were a select and reasonably small party. I could not resist telling them a cautionary tale. During the war in North Africa, I flew in hot weather across the Egyptian sand sea in a light single-engine aircraft. The engine oil began to boil, requiring an immediate forced landing. Looking down, I saw nothing but large dunes, getting bigger as we went down. Tensed for the inevitable disaster, we instead made a perfect landing on a smooth surface. The dunes had marched away, perhaps centuries before, but had left their outlines clearly mosaicked in the flat surface of fine gravel. The moral is that things may not be what they appear.

I spent one evening at a McDonald's with a small group of young scientists from NASA's Jet Propulsion Laboratory in Pasadena. It was fascinating for an old man of eighty-one to listen to their casual talk of navigating a spacecraft two hundred million miles away as easily as an aeroplane. Man had not begun to fly at all when I was born.

Away back in 1927, when I was playing with the properties of dry sand by analyzing the relative proportions of grains of different sizes in samples of natural sands, I discovered that the distributions had a strong tendency to take the form of a hyperbola when plotted on a logarithmic scale. In other words, the "tail" proportions decreased exponentially. As this was contrary to traditional ideas about random distributions, very little notice was taken of the discovery.

Forty years later, Ole Barndorff-Nielsen, professor of theoretical statistics at Aarhus University in Denmark, found that the same hyperbolic distribution occurred in other fields. He invited me to Aarhus in 1977, and again in 1978, this time with Plankie. During the latter visit, the University of Aarhus conferred on me the honorary degree of Doctor of Science at their annual ceremony. Her Majesty Queen Margrethe II was present throughout. I was introduced to her and we had a little chat on two occasions. I found that she was also a Cambridge graduate. Plankie and I greatly enjoyed those Denmark visits and remain grateful to our chief hosts, Professors Ole Barndorff-Nielsen and Jens Tyge Möller. Thanks to the latter, we saw a good deal of Jutland.

Six years later, in 1984, we were once more in Aarhus, the occasion being an international symposium on deserts and desert sands organized by Ole and his staff. I gave a talk in which I was able to clarify the puzzling differences between the transport of solids by winds and by water. I met a number of former acquaintances, in particular from Israel and the United States.

My talks with Ole Barndorff-Nielsen stimulated me to think more about randomness in general. This led me to look for random distributions whose variate consisted of discrete, indivisible additive units so as to forbid any arbitrariness. The most readily available distribution of this kind is a dictionary. The relative frequencies of words of n letters, where n is the variate, is entirely random. I analyzed dictionaries of English, Anglo-Saxon, French, Danish, Hungarian, Arabic, and Sanskrit. Unbiased sampling was done by taking the top and bottom words of every column of the dictionary. Analyzing this sample of several thousand words, I found that the numbers of letters followed the same hyperbolic distribution that I had found for natural sands. The results were published in the *Proceedings of the Royal Society* in 1983, some fifty years after my work with sand distributions.

Precise measurements of random distributions in many diverse fields give the same result. The frequencies of occurrence decay exponentially. For instance, I found that the number of spilt lead shot scattered on the floor decreases exponentially with distance from the point of spillage. As no other widespread pattern of like precision has been found, the facts suggest tentatively the existence of an unrecognized law of nature. Mathematicians, however, on no precise physical evidence, firmly reject the idea. This seems to me to imply that "the facts must be wrong for they disagree with traditional theory." I catch a glimpse of Lewis Carroll's Red Queen here.

One part of the world I had never seen was the Arctic, so Plankie and I took a holiday cruise there in 1977. We first flew to Bergen, which I had visited several times in earlier days, always arriving by sea. It had been the starting point for rail trips to skiing holidays in winter and summer climbing trips in the mountains of Jotunheim. Now it was to be the starting point for our Arctic cruise.

The Norwegians run a mail service up their long coast, as far north as Spitzbergen during the summer. The seven-hundred-mile voyage up the coast is peculiar in that one rarely views the open sea. The nippy little ship twisted and turned through a maze of grass-covered, uninhabited islands. One realized how German battleships had been able to lie hidden there during the Second World War. Crossing the Arctic Circle, we called at Narvik. An ore train from the Swedish iron mountains, just across the border, came in as we landed. We visited the Allied war cemetery for those killed during the attempted defense of Narvik.

Before reaching North Cape, the ship headed due north into the Arctic Ocean in calm, cloudless weather. The weather remained that way for the entire twelve-day trip, and the air at deck level was surprisingly warm. We British and the Norwegians have a lot to thank the Gulf Stream for. Spitzbergen lay another nine hundred miles north. It is the biggest island in the archipelago of Svalbard, most of which is ice covered. Spitzbergen is mountainous, with large areas of bare ground. Svalbard has a Norwegian governor, or administrator, who lives in the Norwegian coal-mining settlement of Longyearbyen. The Russians run another mining settlement on a neighboring fjord. They share an emergency airstrip.

We spent a day in Longyearbyen. There was a church, a school, and a shop-cum–post office. A row of newish villas had been built along the far side of the little valley, and the sewer line from each villa ran on stilts above ground over the permafrost. There were few signs of active mining going on. No doubt it is mostly done in the winter when there can be nothing else to do in the dark. The staff serve on two-year contracts. They are not allowed to stay longer, for mental health reasons. Our ship brought a new consignment of men and their families, and took on board the leavers, who all seemed fit and lively in spite of their two winters frozen in twilight darkness. Plankie and I went for a walk over the permafrost tundra with its tiny alpine saxifages, which grow for only two months of the year.

On leaving, the ship went round to the other fjord and gave a toot of greeting, which was answered by the Russians. I suspect that those two lonely settlements are maintained more for diplomatic than for economic reasons.

We sailed on northward along the coast for quite a way, passing various relics. There was an abandoned, burnt-out coal mine and the mooring mast for the airship of the disastrous Nobile expedition. On one occasion the ship nosed into a narrow fjord where an Arctic glacier overhung the water. Seals were basking asleep on miniature icebergs that had broken off. To my old-fashioned astonishment, the ship turned round in its own length without moving forward or back. It had a transverse bow propeller and so was nimbler than a car.

There is a great population of sea birds around Spitzbergen. The most conspicuous are the little auks, amusing little birds that swarm on the water surface. At any alarm they all instantly disappear downward. Oddly, I seldom if ever saw one of them resurface. The only mammals there, apart from humans, are the seals and the polar bears who eat them. The bears were then in most people's minds because, not more than two weeks earlier, a group of students asleep in a tent some miles from Longyearbyen had been awakened by a scuffling sound outside. One of them, creeping out to investigate, had been dragged away and eaten by a bear, while the others, being unarmed, could do nothing. So we were on the lookout for polar bears, but we saw no signs of any.

The sun at midnight was a little higher in the sky than it is at midday in an English winter. Finally, the horizon ahead began to get curiously white, and soon we were up against the last frontier of the world, an endless wall of ice. We were then beyond latitude 82° N, with the North Pole only five hundred miles away. The north coast of Alaska, on the other side over the top of the world, was only another thousand miles farther on. But for the ice, our ship could have made the pole in a mere day and a half.

The next year, 1978, Plankie and I were invited to Jerusalem by the International Association of Sedimentologists to take part in their Tenth Congress, at which they kindly awarded me their Sorby Medal. The meeting was during July, the off-season, and therefore happily free of tourists. I had some misgivings as to how well Plankie would adapt to the outdoor daytime temperatures—around 40°C (100°-110°F)—and the dazzling sun. With so many new and interesting things around, however, the heat was almost forgotten.

Many new excavations had been done in the temple area since my last visit. It was astonishing to see how painstakingly the Roman soldiers had carried out the ordered destruction after the great siege of A.D. 70. Chamber below chamber underground had been so completely filled with broken stonework that there was hardly room for another small piece. To me, Jerusalem was of far greater interest for my having read Josephus's book *The Jewish War*, in which he described in detail the horrific siege. He had taken part himself and so knew of it firsthand. The city walls, though renovated much later by the Turks, remained largely as they had been.

Jerusalem is a first-class example of the "red queen ability." After the long siege, followed by the deliberate destruction and slaughter or exile of the surviving inhabitants, coupled with the lack of written records, it is impossible that any of the now-accepted sites of Christ's birth, execution, or burial can be authentic. It is even more impossible that the humble manger and rock-hewn vault of the Gospels could have been the bejewelled extravagances now shown in Bethlehem and Jerusalem, or that the last journey to Calvary was cramped into the confines of a single church. Yet generations of pious pilgrims have believed these things, at least with half their minds.

The True Cross was discovered at the politically convenient time that Constantine made Christianity the official religion. The relic was kept by the bishops of Jerusalem, who very profitably sold pieces of it. The people of Christendom must certainly have realized that the one True Cross was producing far more wood than it could ever have contained, yet they went on buying. One might define a miracle as an impossibility it is pleasant or convenient to believe.

A lot of piety is needed if one is to be exalted by the modern show of Christianity in Jerusalem. On my previous visits to the Church of the Holy Sepulchre, the whole place stank of urine because of continual "who does what where" disputes between the many quarrelsome sects; they couldn't even agree where to put a loo. Fortunately, the Israeli Jews now in control have enforced sanitation.

The one place where we felt an aura of genuineness was in what is said to be the Garden of Gethsemane. We were alone there. It was so clean and peaceful, and the gnarled, twisted olive trunks looked ancient enough to have been there in Christ's time. It was lovely to think so. Yet Titus's besieging legions, who camped in the area, must surely have needed every scrap of wood for cooking.

We found, as we had expected, the Israelis to be kind, thoughtful hosts, and realists at the same time. Always at war or on the verge of it, both boys and girls were seen in the streets in uniform and carrying rifles. Yet they happily took a coachload of tourists around the war zones. One of the nicest things about the Old City, especially in very hot weather, is the ubiquitous supply of ice-cold orange juice. At most street corners one finds a man standing beside an upright fridge with a squeezer on top.

We went on a coach tour from Jerusalem down the long drop to the Dead Sea, along its western shore and past Masada, the scene of the last siege of the Roman-Jewish war. At the southern end of the Dead Sea the modern highroad rises a little up the mountainside, and we overlooked the delta of old watercourses, now dry and lifeless, and the broad plain of the rift floor. In my mind's eye I saw three very old-fashioned, spindly cars beside a fetid swamp and a young bearded man in scanty clothing who had forced a way down where there had never been a road; down, down, down, from the Red Sea to the mysterious Ghor-es-Safi which had long ago been the land of Sodom and Gomorra. Surely it wasn't possible that young man could be myself, a half century before.

The tour continued past the salt works and on southward along a modern highway through the Negev Desert to the Aqaba arm of the Red Sea. On the shore, next to Aqaba, stands the new Israeli seaport of Elat. I felt the same break of identity when standing on the beach in that busy little town. People were boating and bathing in the clear, sparkling water of the sea. Surely this couldn't be the same beach that was barren, devoid of even a camel track, along which that young man had struggled, car wheels in the sea, years before the state of Israel existed.

The proper point at which to end an autobiography is when it becomes unlikely there will be anything further to narrate. The age of ninety-one seems a good time. There remain a few things to tie up, and perhaps a few thoughts to express.

We left Rickwoods in December 1983. A spacious Victorian house with seven bedrooms, together with nine acres of land, was getting to be too much of a burden. I was eighty-seven, and Plankie had just recovered from a serious illness. Moreover, we were finding a home in the country too isolated.

We bought No. 7 Manor Way, in Blackheath, a suburb of London. With much help from Stephen, the move was surprisingly smooth. Plankie somehow managed to organize a Christmas lunch for the whole family—Stephen and his wife Britt, their three boys, Jane and Guy McKenzie and their two children, Simon and Lucy, Britt's Norwegian mother, Ella, and ourselves. Our new home is a modern semibungalow enclosed within a small walled-in bit of ground. By an odd coincidence it is within two miles of Shooters Hill, where our old home used to be. The main attraction, though, was that it is only ten minutes' walk from Stephen and Britt, and so we no longer feel isolated. In the first spring there, with the family's help, we started on the garden, till then a bare, rubbish-strewn plot. Creepers soon changed the barracks-like look of the boundary walls. We have become well pleased with our new home. Memories of lovely Rickwoods are kept alive thanks to a fine painting by Anthony Cook.

I was surprised and very pleased when, in 1986, Michael Haag told me he would like to reproduce my first book, *Libyan Sands,* published in 1935 and long out of print. It is now on sale again, with an epilogue outlining the war sequel and the creation of the Long Range Desert Group. I was even more surprised and gratified when, the same year, the American Society of Civil Engineers, a formidable body with 150,000 members, published a collection of my scientific papers in book form. This was done to coincide with the celebration of the fiftieth anniversary of their Hydraulics Division and also, incidentally, with my ninetieth birthday.

My lifetime has covered more changes in outlooks and availabilities than occurred in any other like period in history. When I was born, the Great Queen was still reigning, as she had throughout the lives of most of her subjects. She had already given her name to an era and still had another five years to rule. We were proud to be members of the most widespread, richest, and most powerful empire the world had seen. The British navy was kept stronger than the combined fleets of any other three nations, and it effectively policed the world's waterways. There were no overseas communications other than by ship or by submarine cables which we had laid and ourselves controlled. There was no radio of any kind, and of course no television. At home, groups of telephones were joined by a few trunk lines. Even the blaring thing with a trumpet and a listening dog was still to come. There were no spacecraft, no satellites, and no man had yet flown an aircraft. Nuclear physics was unknown, though J. J. Thompson started it the year of my birth by discovering the electron. There were no self-propelled vehicles other than trains, and no tarmac roads. Mr. Macadam was introducing his novel system of water-bound road metal pressed firm by Messrs. Aveling and Porter's steamroller (Aveling was a friend of my father). One walked, rode a horse or bicycle, or went by train carriage or horsedrawn omnibus.

Everything was more staid and formal. Schoolboys had to wear top hats and long-tailed morning coats on Sundays. Visiting cards were exchanged with an elaborate etiquette. It was a world of everlasting perfection. There was no inflation, for the generally accepted gold standard kept financial stability. Prices remained fixed. The two political parties came largely from the same professional class and differed courteously on relatively minor questions of policy.

That life changed with World War I. I served with the volunteer "Kitchener Division." The division did well and we were proud of it. We lived a weird, other-worldly life among shell holes and rotting, fly-covered corpses. We got used to it. At my age I had known no other kind of adult life. We worked for the very urgent present, looking ahead no further than the next hoped-for period of blissful relaxation. Our future seemed unlikely. That life appears to have caused me no lasting harm, but it left me a realist without a reverence for dead bodies, and with a cynical disbelief in the so-called "sanctity of human life," a concept which stems from the monstrous, absurd conceit that Man was made in the image of God. What monumental arrogance on the one hand, and what utter impudence on the other.

Our losses in the First World War were considerable—during eighteen months, my little section, some forty strong, had over sixty casualties. The majority of my friends gradually disappeared and were replaced by new faces. Sometime in the 1920s, it must have been after the first postwar census, I saw in the newspaper a diagram of the United Kingdom age distribution of males. The effect of the 1914–18 war stood out starkly. The regular curve had a great bite taken out of it, centered on my generation. Through the following years the bite has shifted upward, over the hump and down the other side. Now it has all but disappeared off the diagram. Similar diagrams for other West European countries must show the same bite, but for us the lasting effect has been worse. Whereas the Continental countries were all conscriptive, and so lost from the average population, we have never known conscription in Britain, calling instead on volunteers. As a result, the war did not kill off the average of my generation; it took the best, the most responsible, and at the same time the most venturesome elements of all classes. These were the individuals who would have, during mid-century, provided needed stability and common sense to our country. To a lesser extent, the loss must have extended to the next generation.

My main urge, from boyhood onward, was curiosity. This was often strong enough to stimulate active steps to satisfy it. Along with this, there has been a vague longing to discover something new, something previously unknown. At first the curiosity was how my toys were made, and with a push from my father, how I might mend them myself. I was told, "Try it and see." Then came an intense curiosity about ancient times, probably the result of Old Testament history lessons. In Egypt, with so many ancient sites strewn about the Middle East but difficult to reach, the call became "go there and see." That started my curiosity about the Model-T Fords as a means of getting there cross-country or along old camel tracks where no car had ever been. That led to the huge satisfaction of desert exploration—far beyond the limits previously set by the biological endurance of the camel—of seeing landscapes no humans had visited since Stone Age times. It also led my interest to veer from man-made things to natural processes, initially to those processes responsible for the vast, organized, and moving forms of the desert dune systems. Later, the same interest widened to cover the action of similar processes underwater, and to many kindred problems.

Being an amateur, a free lance who had never held any academic post or had any professional status, I had the rather unusual advantage of considering problems with an open mind, unbiased by traditional textbook ideas that had remained untested against facts. I had the further advantage that the sort of problems that interested me did not involve expensive or elaborate apparatus. I could design and make what I needed.

In a talk I had with my sister Enid some years before her death, she said with, for her, unusual diffidence, "I think, don't you, we both in our different ways have a bit of genius." I said, "The difference between us is that you are interested in people and I am more interested in things." On reflection, I have been more involved with "things"—with science and exploration—but people have been an important part of my life as well.

Index

Aarhus University, Denmark, 190–91
Abu Dhabi, 182–83
Abyssinia (Ethiopia), Italian army in, 120–21
Acclimatization, 114
Afghanistan, 74
Africa. *See* Egypt; Expeditions
Agave, 112
Ainu tribe, Japan, 111
Alger, Ethel (mother), 1, 5, 81
Alger, Harold (uncle), 82, 83
Alger, William Henry (grandfather), 1, 83
Algeria, 156–57
Algiers, 156–57
Almasy, Laslo, 155
Amani, Tanganyika (Tanzania), 112, 113
American Society of Civil Engineers, 197
Amsterdam, 149
Angkor, 97–100
Angkor Wat temple, 98–100
Ankara, Turkey, 122

Ants, 8, 112
Approach to problems: and academic bias, 170, 199–200; in desert driving, 59; by engineers and physicists, 161–62; with German shell, 25; with solids in liquid, 154–55. *See also* Experiments
Aqaba, Gulf of, 57, 59
Arctic cruise, 192–94
Army service. *See* Royal Army
Astrofix. *See* Navigation
Aswan Dam, 87
Automobiles: family Cadillac, 13–14; in Far East, 94, 98; in Libyan Desert, 115, 117, 121, 126; Light Car Patrols, 121, 124; Morris car, 49, 54. *See also* Ford vehicles; Long Range Desert Patrol
Awards, 89, 184, 185, 194

Bagnold, Alexander Burns (Uncle Lexy), 3, 13
Bagnold, Arthur Henry (father), 2, 4–11, 15, 81, 82, 141

Bagnold, Clara (aunt), 3
Bagnold, Eliza (grandmother), 3
Bagnold, Enid (sister), 5–6, 8, 16, 146–47, 200
Bagnold, Jane (daughter), 153–54, 169–70, 196
Bagnold, Michael Edward (grandfather), 2
Bagnold, Ralph: awards, 89, 184, 185, 194; childhood, 1, 7–11; early interest in science, 8–9, 17–18; education, 11–12, 18–21, 35–40; health, 79, 100–101, 104, 132, 137; marriage and children, 147, 150, 153, 169, 196; publications, 106–7, 191, 197. See also Approach; Experiments; Expeditions
Bagnold, Stephen (son), 150, 169, 170, 196–97
Bakhtiari Mountains (Persian Gulf), 186
Ball, John, 70
Balloon barrage, 146
Bandits, 73, 84, 85, 87, 89, 95
Bangalor Torpedo, 27
Bangkok, 96–98
Banihal Pass, India, 77
Baring, Evelyn (Lord Cromer), 50
Barker, R.E., 46, 123
Barndorff-Nielsen, Ole, 190–91
Battle of Amiens, 33
Beaches, action of waves on, 146
Beggars, in China, 92
Ben Gurion, David, 157
Bernoulli, Daniel, 176
Black-and-Tans, 43
Bombing of London, 145–46
Boston, 167–68
Boustead, Hugh (Sir Hugh), 85, 183–84
Brennan, Louis, 6, 14–15

Brennan torpedo, 6
British Empire, reflections on, 92, 197–99
British Expeditionary Force, in France, 23–34
British Indian government, 183
British Troops in Egypt (BTE), 49–51, 63, 64, 120, 122–23; and LRDG, 121–22, 123, 126, 128, 138
Buddha, 96, 97
Budge, Wallis, 5
Buraimi Oasis, 182–83
Burnard, Jack, 83–84
Burnard, Lawrence, 82, 83
Burnard, Robert, 81
Burnard and Alger, firm of, 1, 81–84
Buttress tree, 98–99

Cable, 31–33, 76–77, 123. See also Communications
Cadillac, 13–14
Cairo, 85; during World War II, 119–20, 121, 122, 136, 137, 140
Caius College (Cambridge), 34, 35–41
California, 146, 189–90
Cambodia, 97–100
Cambridge, 34, 35–41
Camels, 88–89
Canals, in Flanders (Belgium), 26
Canton, China, 92–93
Cars. See Automobiles
Cataract Canyon, 177–79
Cattedown Wharves, Ltd., 82, 83–84
Cattewater Inlet, 81
Cavalry, 30
Cavan, Lord (Earl of Cavan), 26, 28, 31
Chad, French army in, 131–36
Chatham, 4–6
Chester, 149, 150

Chevrolet, 126
China, 91–94
Chloroform, as solvent, 154–55
Churchill, Winston, 35
Clayton, Pat, 71, 115, 125–26, 127, 128, 129, 131, 155
Climbing, mountain, 69–70, 112–14
Cold research station, U.S. army, 184–85
Coldspring House, Jamaica, 7–9
Collins, Michael, 44–46
Colorado River, 165, 177–79
Communications: cable, 31–33, 76–77, 123; changes in 197; radio, 76–77, 127, 131, 136; telegraph, 139–40; telephone, 11; World War I, 31–33; World War II, 123, 131, 136, 139–40
Concrete, childhood interest in, 5, 9
Consulting: in Abu Dhabi, 182–84; in Iran, 185–87; in Iraq, 181–82; in Kuwait, 158–59; in Qatar, 150; in the U.S., 166–67
Cook's Nile Steamers, 4–5
Copper violin, 17–18
Council of Liverpool University, 150
Creagh, General, 122
Cubby (dog), 49, 73, 74, 80
Curragh, Ireland, 43–48
Curzon, George Nathaniel, 74

Dalgas (Danish mining engineer), 27–28
Darb el Arba'in, 89
Dartmoor, 15–16, 19–20
Dead Sea, 57, 60, 61, 195–96
De Gaulle, Charles, 133–35
Dehydration, 65–66, 159–60
Denmark, 190–91
Desert. See Expeditions; Long Range Desert Group; Sand dunes

Desert warfare. See Long Range Desert Group
Devonport, 1, 6
Dispersion of solids in liquid, 161–64. See also Experiments
Dobie (doctor), 30, 150
D'Ornano (French commander), 132–34
Dunes. See Sand dunes
Durand Line, 74

East Fork River (Wyoming), installation at, 173–77
East India Company, 2
Eboué (governor of Chad), 131–33
Eden, Anthony, 128, 138
Egypt: ancient ruins of, 5, 52–54, 140–41; father in, 4–5; FDA, 54, 55; invaded by Italy, 129; Ministry of Agriculture, 63; stationed in (1926–29), 49–71; stationed in (1939–44), 119–41; strange tribes in, 60, 61. See also Expeditions; Long Range Desert Group
Egyptian Desert Institute, 155–56
Egyptian Desert Survey, 70, 71, 155
Egyptian Frontier Administration (FDA), 54, 55
El Din, Prince Kemal, 62, 64, 70, 115
Electricity, 7, 12
Emery, Walter, 140–41
Emmett, Bill, 171, 176, 177
Engineering degree, 37–38
England: bombing of, 145–46; in 1902, 10
English Channel, 146
Expeditions, desert: accounting system for, 85; articles written about, 85; dehydration, 65–66, 159–60; Great Sand Sea (Libya) in 1929, 62, 63–65; in 1930, 65–66; Libyan

Desert, in 1938, 114–18; navigation, 68–69; packing for, 66–68; to Petra, 57–59; rules for, 67; Selima Sand Sheet (Sudan) in 1928, 63; in 1932, 84–89; Sinai, 54–61. *See also* Japan; Long Range Desert Group; Newfoundland

Experiments: action of sea waves on beaches, 146; dispersion of solids in liquid, 161–64; East Fork River installation, 173–77; physics of blown sand, 103–7, 117; random distributions, 190–92; rotating drum, 163–64; sediment transport in water, 154–55, 161–64, 165–66, 171, 173–77; shear and friction, 154, 163–64; water flume, 154–55; wave tank, 146; wind tunnel, 103–7, 117

Explosives, 21, 25, 27–28

Farming, in Israel, 157–58
Farouk, King, 155–56
Fat-tailed sheep, 136
Feiran oasis, Egypt, 56–57
Fellow of the Royal Society (FRS), 91, 145
Filham House, 83
Flanders (Belgium), 23–34
Flume, 154–55. *See also* Experiments
Ford vehicles, 54–55, 57, 59, 60–63, 64–69, 84–89
Foreign Office (London), 88
Fort Lamy (Njamina), 132
France: Chad province, 131–36; college trips to, 40–41; French Indochina, 98–100; World War I, 23–34; World War II, 122, 123, 131–36
Francis, John, 146
Freyberg, General, 126
Fuad, King, 50, 155

Garden of Gethsemane, 195
Geological Society of America, 185
Geological Society of London, 185
Germany, 26, 122, 123, 139
Gilf Kebir (Great Cliff), 115, 117, 129
GOC, 44–45, 85
Gold, at Farouk's palace, 156
Gordon, Charles, 4–5
Grand Canyon of the Colorado River, 169–170
Grand Erg Occidental, 156–57
Graziani, Rodolfo, 123, 131
Great Britain, 10, 92, 145–46, 197–99. *See also* British Troops in Egypt; Ireland
Great Sand Sea (Libya), 62–69
Green River, Utah, 177
Gulf of Aqaba, 59
Guraan people, Chad, 89
Gyro truck, 14–15

Hance, Bill, 155
Harding-Newman, Rupert, 85, 126
Haynes, Vance, 66
Heat stroke, 159–60
Hebuterne region, France, 29
History, interest in, 38–39, 140–41
H.M.S. *Velox*, 47–48
Hobart, General, 120, 121
Holland (Netherlands), 149
Holy Land tour, 194–95
Hong Kong, 91–94
Hopkins, Major, 24
Hopkinson, G.F. (Hoppy), 37, 39
Hor Aha, tomb of, 141
Horner, Nils, 94
Horses: army use of, 20, 30; Enid and, 8, 16
Hyde Park, Enid's cow in, 147
Hydraulics laboratories, 170–71

Imperial College, 108, 146, 154
India, 2, 63, 73–80
Indochina, 95–100
Indus River, 78
Inman, Douglas, 146
Institution of Electrical Engineers, 6–7
International Association of Sedimentologists, 194
Iran, 185–87
Iraq, 181–82
Ireland: honeymoon in, 147–48; stationed in, 43–48
Irrigation systems, ancient Egyptian, 53
Israel, 157–58, 194–96
Italian army in Libya, 87–88, 120–21, 123–25, 129, 131

Jamaica, 7–9
Japan, Solar Eclipse Expedition to, 108–12
Jardine Matheson, firm of, 93, 94
Jarvis (governor of Sinai), 55, 57, 59
Jebel Usdam, Egypt, 61
Jerusalem, tour of, 194–96
"Jesus gun" prank, 37
Jones, Roderick (brother-in-law), 147
Jones, Tucker (nephew), 81

Kármán, Theodor von, 104, 156
Kashmir, India, 77–78
Keynes, John Maynard, 38
Khartoum, 4–5, 131
Khassadars, 75
Khedives, of Egypt, 49–51
Khufu's Great Pyramid, 53
Kilimanjaro, 108, 112–114
Kinematics, and fluid, 162–63. See also Experiments

Kipling, Rudyard, 147
Kirkpatrick, Tommy, 39, 40–41 74–75, 108, 112–14
Kitchener, Horatio Herbert ("Old Kitch"), 4, 23–34
Kufra oasis, 87, 129, 133–36
Kutum, Sudan, 88
Kuwait Oil Company, 158–60
Kweiwa, 94–95

Labyrinth Canyon, 178
Lagia Oasis, 89
Las Vegas, Nevada, 168–69
Lattimore, Owen, 94
Leclerc, Colonel (Philippe de Haut Clocque), 133, 134
Leopold, Luna, 165–180; East Fork River experiment, 173–77
Leopold, Madelyn, 170
Libya, 62, 63–66, 87–88, 114–48. See also Italian army in Libya; Long Range Desert Group
Libyan Desert. See Libya
Libyan Sands: Travel in a Dead World, 85, 197
Light Car Patrols, 121, 124
Lloyd, Lord, 51
Logarithms, and random distribution, 106
London, 10, 12; bombing of, 145–46
Long Range Desert Group (LRDG): conception of, 121–28; first patrols of, 128–30; at Kufra, 133–36; mapping by, 139; Murzuk raid, 131–34; praise for, 137; and SAS, 138–39
Longyearbyen, Norway, 192–94
LRDG. See Long Range Desert Group
Lyminge, 146, 148, 149

Maan, Egypt, 59
McKenzie, Guy (son-in-law), 196

Malvern College, 18–19
Manor House, 6
Maps, desert, 134, 139
Margrethe II, Queen of Denmark, 190–91
Mars, possible dunes on, 189–90
Medicine, 79
Mesopotamia, 181–82
Middle East, consulting in, 150, 158–59, 181–84, 185–87
Miller, John, 167–68
Milwaukee, Wisconsin, 185
Mines (explosives), in World War I, 27–28
Mitford, Teddy, 129
Model-A Ford, 66–69, 84–89
Model-T Ford, 54–55, 57, 59, 60–63, 64–66
Moors and bogs, 16–17
Morris car, 49, 54
Moslem pilgrim trade, 108–9
"Mosquito army," 138
Mountain climbing, 69–70, 112–14
Mountain of the Lawgivers, 55
Mountbatten, Lord Louis, 51, 146
Mount Serbal, Egypt, 55
Mummies, 5
Murray, George, 70, 155, 160
Murray-Levick, G., 107–8
Murzuk, oases in Libya, 131, 132–33

NASA (National Aeronautics and Space Administration), 189–90
National Academy of Sciences (U.S.), 184
National Velvet, 6
Natural gas, in Kuwait, 158
Navigation, 68–69, 127
Negev Desert, 196

Newbold, Douglas, 66, 70, 131–32, 133
Newfoundland expedition, 107–8
New Zealanders, in LRDG, 126–27, 128, 129, 136
Nile steamers, 4–5
Norway, 192–94

Oases: Buraimi, 182–83; Feiran, 56–57; Kufra, 87, 129, 133–36; Lagia, 89; Murzuk, 131, 132–33
Oberg (young Swede at Kweiwa), 94–95
O'Conner, Dick, 134–35, 143
OETA (Occupied Enemy Territory Administration), 134–35
Oil industry, consulting for: 148–51, 159–60, 182–84, 185–87. *See also* Shell Oil Company
Oriel, John, 148, 149, 150
Orient Express, 168
Overgrazing, in Iraq, 181–82

Palladium, 185
Palm Desert, California, 189
Pasha, Peake, 57, 59, 60, 61
Passchendaele battle, Belgium, 31–32
Penrose Gold Medal, 185
Permafrost, Arctic, 192–93
Persian Gulf, consulting in, 150, 158–59, 181–84, 185–87
Perspex, laboratory material, 154–55
Petra, 57, 59–60
Philips, Charles E.S., 17–18
Physics of Blown Sand and Desert Dunes, The, 106–7
Pinedale, Wyoming, 174–75, 179
Pipes, childhood interest in, 8–9
Piracy, 182–83

Pirate Coast, 182–83
Plank, Dorothy (wife "Plankie"), 147–48, 179–80, 196–97
Plankie. *See* Plank, Dorothy
Plymouth, 5, 81
Polar bears, 193
Prendergast, Guy, 70, 85, 137
Prince Kemal el Din, 62, 64, 70, 115
Prince of Wales (Edward VIII), 30–31
Probability, interest in, 77, 190–92
Publications, 85, 106–7, 191, 197
Public Schools Exploring Society, 107–8
Pyramid, Khufu's Great, 53

Qatar, 150
Qattara Depression, 122
Queen Margrethe II of Denmark, 190–91

Radio, 76–77, 127, 131, 136. *See also* Communications
Raft trips: Colorado River, 177–79; Loire, 40–41
Rail travel in U.S., 167–68
Random distributions, theories of, 190–92
"Red queen ability," 187, 192, 194
Religion: in Egypt, 53–54; at Holy Land sites, 194–95; in India, 74–75; and Mecca pilgrims, 108–9; observations on, 114, 148, 186–87, 198
Rickwoods, 153–54, 196–97
Rivers: Colorado, 177–79; Loire, 40–41; transport rate of solids in, 165–66, 173–74
Roads, unusual, 54, 77

Rotating drum, 163–64. *See also* Experiments
Royal Air Force (RAF), 137, 138
Royal Army, service in: academy, 19; China and Far East, 91–101; Egypt, 49–63, 64–71, 119–43; engineers, joined, 20; family tradition, 2–3, 91; father in, 2, 4–7, 8, 10, 30; France, 23–34; India, 63–64, 73–80; Ireland, 43–48; rank, 23, 63, 131, 137, 139; signals, instructor for, 84; signals, transfer to, 30; World War I, 20–34; World War II, 119–43. *See also* Long Range Desert Group
Royal Corps of Signals, 48
Royal Engineers. *See* Royal Army
Royal Geographical Society, 84, 89, 114–15
Royal Military Academy at Woolrich, 4, 19–20
Rutherford, Sir Ernest, 18

Sailing, in Hong Kong, 92
Sampling, transport rate of solids, 173. *See also* Experiments
Sand dunes: of Earth and Mars, 189–90; encroaching on oil fields, 159, 181–87; Grand Erg Occidental, 156–57; movement of, 66; odd behavior and shapes of, 103–4; vibrating, 118; and wind tunnel experiments, 105–6, 117. *See also* Expeditions
Sandford, Kenneth, 85
Sand storms, measuring wind during, 117
Saqqara, Egypt, ancient tombs at, 140–41

School of Military Engineering at Chatham, 4, 5, 20–21
School of Signals at Catterick, 84
Science, early interest in, 17–18
Scientific publications, 85, 106–7, 191, 197
Scripps Institute of Oceanography, 146
Sediment transport, 154–55, 161–64, 165–66, 171, 173–77. See also Experiments
Selima Sand Sheet (Sudan), 63, 88–89
Senussi tribes, 87, 121
Shafiullah (Indian valet), 74, 80
Shaw, Bill: on 1930s expeditions, 70, 84, 85, 87–89; with LRDG, 125–26, 127, 128, 131, 139
Shearer, John, 128
Shear stress, 154, 163–64. See also Experiments
Shell Oil Company: aided Sudan expedition, 84, 88; job with Shell Refining and Marketing Company, 148–51. See also Oil industry
Shooters Hill, 10, 11
Siam (Thailand), 96–98
Signals branch of engineers: instructor for, 84; transfer to, 30. See also Royal Army
Singapore, 95–96
Skibisky, Herb, 179
Slave route, ancient, 89
Smell, sense of, 88–89
Smith, Sir Arthur, 124
Solar Eclipse Expedition, 108–12
Sorby Award, 194
Special Air Service (SAS), 138–39
Sphinx, Great, 52
Stirling, David, 138

Stone Age implements, 117–18
Stonework: at Angkor Wat, 99–100; at temple of Zozer, 52–53
Stradivarius violins, 17–18
Strait of Hormuz, 182
Stratton, F. J. M., 23, 31–34, 35–37, 40, 107, 108–12
Stream energy, 176. See also Experiments
Sudan, 63, 84–89
Sudan Civil Service, 85, 87
Sun compass, 63, 68–69

Tanks (army vehicles), 29–30
Technology: architecture, 53, 93–94; automobile, 10, 13–14; fascination with, 17–18, 190, 197–98; gyro truck, 14–15; ships, 4–5, 7, 193; steam, 4–5, 7, 10, 11; tanks, 29–30; windmill, 12; x-rays, 79–80. See also Automobiles; Communications; Transportation
Teheran, 185–87
Telegraph, 4, 139–40. See also Communications
Telephone, 11
Tibesti Mountains, 133, 136
Times (London), 85
Tombs, ancient Egyptian, 140–41
Tools, 9, 10–11, 141, 154
Torpedoes, 6, 27
Tourism, in Holy Land, 194–95
Tovey, Admiral, 47–48
Transjordan, 57–61
Transportation: air, 63; animal, 12, 24, 30; desert, 62–63; military, 24, 29–30; rail, 13, 31, 96, 167–68; ships, 4, 5, 96, 149–50, 170. See also Automobiles; Expeditions; Technology

Transport rate of solids, 154–55, 161–64, 165–66, 171, 173–77. *See also* Experiments

Trench warfare, 23–24, 25, 26–29

Truth, reflections on, 186–87

"Try it and see" approach. *See* Approach

Turkey, 115, 122

United Arab Emirates, 182–83

United States, 149, 166–68, 174–77, 184–85

United States Geological Survey, 165–66, 170–71

Uweinat (mountain pass), 87, 115, 121, 123

Vegetation, on Kilimanjaro, 112–13

Vichy government, 131, 132

Violins, 17–18

Von Kármán, Theodor, 104, 156

Walker, Eliza Larkins (grandmother), 2

War Office, 120

Warren Prize, 184

Warren Wood, 10–11, 35, 141, 145

Washington, D.C., 166–67

Water flow, knowledge of, 162–63. *See also* Experiments

Wave action experiments, 146

Wavell, Archibald, 119–20, 122, 124–25, 128, 131, 137–38, 142–43

Wave tank, 146

Waziristan, India, 78–79

Weapons: naval guns, 11; Pathan Knife, 76; primitive field gun, 76; tanks, 29–30; torpedoes, 6, 27

Wells, H.G., 103

Whish-hunter legend, 16–17

White, C. M., 104

Wigram, Kenneth, 75–77

Wildlife, 88, 193

Williams, Garnet, 171, 177

Wilson, Henry Maitland (Jumbo), 121, 124, 126, 128

Windmill, 12

Wind tunnel, 104–6, 117. *See also* Experiments

Wind velocity, 104

Wireless stations, in Ireland, 44

Wollaston Medal, 85

Woolwich Arsenal, 141–42

World War I: beginning of, 20–21; in Egypt, 50–51; in France and Flanders, 23–34; impact of, 198–99; postwar students, 36, 37–38

World War II, 119–43. *See also* Long Range Desert Group

Wyoming, 174–77

X-rays, 79–80

Ypres, Belgium, 25–26, 28, 31–32

Yser Canal, 26

Zaharoff, Basil, 4

Zaid (Sheikh), 183, 184

Zozer, temple of, 52–53

Zungi (Indian Tribal leader), 76–77